Handbook *for* Writing Proposals

SECOND EDITION

Robert J. Hamper and L. Sue Baugh

New York Chicago San Francisco Lisbon London
Madrid Mexico City Milan New Delhi San Juan
Seoul Singapore Sydney Toronto

The *McGraw-Hill* Companies

1 2 3 4 5 6 7 8 9 10   DOC/DOC   1 9 8 7 6 5 4 3 2 1 0

MHID   0-07-174648-X
ISBN   978-0-07-174648-9

McGraw-Hill books are available at special quantity discounts to use as premiums and sales promotions, or for use in corporate training programs. To contact a representative, please e-mail us at bulksales@mcgraw-hill.com.

This book is printed on acid-free paper.

* * * * *

To Norm and Mary, who supported us throughout the development of this book.

To the entrepreneurs who risk it all to achieve their dreams and to the corporate managers who are the heart and soul of their companies.

* * * * *

Contents

Introduction

Today, a record number of people are going into business for themselves, either on their own or with others. To survive, they must learn quickly how to attract and win clients. In the corporate world, more companies are chasing fewer dollars. Corporate managers and marketing/sales staff need to prepare superior proposals to win client business.

If you have launched your own business, are a manager in any size corporation, or simply want to improve your proposal process, *Handbook for Writing Proposals* is for you. In this book, you will discover how to find bids, how to evaluate which bids you should pursue, and how to develop winning proposals, including personal client presentations.

In this second edition, we provide more detailed information on how to prepare budgets and time/cost estimates. We also include tips on using international business English. In today's global market, your proposal may be read by managers or executives who are not native English speakers. As an added feature, the second edition offers downloadable forms that can be edited and customized for your company's use.

How to Use This Book

You can work straight through this book or find the chapter that gives you the specific information you need. We cover eight essential topics:

1. *How do you know where to start?* Chapter 1 explains that the real starting point is developing your marketing strategy. What business are you in and why are you in it? By knowing your business strategy, you will be able to target clients and bids that support your strategy and increase your chances of building a successful business.

2. *What is the proposal process?* Chapter 2 provides an overview of the 9-step proposal process. This chapter briefly describes the steps you need to take from the moment the request for proposal (RFP) arrives through the final proposal production and client presentation stages.

3. *How do you select and choose a proposal team?* Chapters 1 and 3 give you guidelines for making a bid/no-bid decision to avoid going after too many bids or pursuing bids you have little chance of winning. Chapter 3 also shows you how to build an effective proposal team. The final section in this chapter describes how to find market research information easily and quickly. We provide a list of major databases available to any firm.

4. *What is your unique selling point (USP)?* What do you have to offer the client that will make you stand out from your competition? Chapter 4 discusses ways to find the client's stated and unstated problems and needs that can inspire your unique selling point.

5. *How do you create the best program design?* Clients want to know what you can do for them and why you, rather than your competition, should be hired for the job. Chapter 5 explains in detail how you can develop a solid, powerful program design that shows potential clients that you understand their problems and needs, have the best solution for their situation, and are the best company for the job.

6. *What goes into a complete proposal?* The body of the proposal is only part of what makes a winning document. Chapter 6 shows you how to develop an effective cover or transmittal letter and an executive summary and how to establish a format for your proposal design. Clients must be able to find their way through your proposal documents easily.

7. *How do you use tables and graphics?* With today's design software, even one-person companies can produce impressive

documents. Chapter 7 focuses on producing your proposal, particularly the effective use of tables and graphics to support your text.

8. *How do you make an effective client presentation?* Translating your written proposal into a winning presentation is as much art as science. Chapter 8 covers the process from initial planning, organization, and practice to the actual presentation itself—setting up for success and handling troublesome questions from the client. This chapter helps you make the best impression on the client.

Special Features of This Book

Whether you are new at writing proposals or an experienced hand, you will find these features helpful:

- *Forms and checklists:* Each chapter offers simple forms, checklists, and questions to stimulate your thinking and help you develop forms tailored to your particular company.
- *Samples of proposal formats:* Throughout the book, you will find samples of refusal letters, cover letters, proposal tables of contents, budget forms, title pages, executive summaries, résumé boilerplates, and proposals themselves.
- *Samples of tables and graphics:* Chapter 7 provides clear examples of how and why different types of graphics are used and when to use them.
- *Summaries of key points:* Throughout the book, we summarize the key points discussed to provide a quick reference list.
- *Downloadable forms:* These forms, which can be edited and customized for your company, are available on the McGraw-Hill Web site. Go to www.mhprofessional.com/writingproposals.
- *Added writing help:* Today, many businesspeople in the United States and in U.S. firms abroad speak English as a second language. To help you tailor your writing to the needs of all your readers, we have included a brief guide to international business English, along with guides to frequently confused words and frequently misspelled words. These guides are found in the Appendixes.

Plan, Prepare, Practice

The business climate today is full of risks and opportunities. You need every competitive edge possible. *Handbook for Writing Proposals* was designed to help you plan, prepare, and practice to create a successful business. We hope this book helps you minimize your risks and make the most of your opportunities in this rapidly changing world. We wish you the best.

1

Where to Begin

Nicolle Herras, a manager at Integrated Medical Systems, studied a request for proposal that had arrived on her desk that morning. Everett Hospital, a local care facility, had a growing number of patients who did not speak English. The hospital staff was having trouble finding translators for all the different languages the patients spoke. This lack of communication resulted in poor treatment and follow-up efforts. The hospital management was seeking a high-tech solution to the problem.

Ms. Herras called her boss, Mr. Hardin Tagore, and told him about the request.

"Mr. Tagore, this is right in line with our revised company mission to develop interactive communication interfaces. We've got the systems, expertise, and databases to solve their problems. And I think we have an excellent shot at follow-up projects working with their satellite care facilities. Our competitors wouldn't be able to offer as complete a package."

"I know Everett's IT director," Mr. Tagore said. "He's wanted to update their in-house and external communication facilities for some time. Let's meet later this week after I get a bid/no-bid decision on this RFP. Meanwhile, see if you can put together a good proposal team."

Ms. Herras had only one reservation in going after the job. Two of the people she had in mind for the proposal team were new hires. They had limited experience in developing proposals at the corporate level. Well, she thought, this will be their chance to learn.

* * *

George Lee's marketing firm had been hit hard by a downturn in the economy. Searching for new business and new ideas, he noticed hundreds of little "green" companies springing up across the country that had no idea how to get their message across to potential customers. Here was a niche his company could fill. He explained his idea to his writing staff.

"We can target green energy and home renovation firms—we know the most about those fields. Our proposal has to convince these companies that putting money into targeted marketing materials can yield big returns. We have experience with some of the green energy fields and the target customers for this niche. Let's propose a partnership that combines the green companies' products and our media savvy."

*   *   *

Linda Valdez spread the requests for proposals across her desk. Her information technology company was new to the marketplace, so it made sense to try for any and all jobs her firm might win. There was a telecom company contract for market data analyses, a municipal study to examine traffic pattern flows to improve safety measures, and a corporate contract to develop inventory software for the company's international offices.

Her staff would be stretched a little thin on the corporate job, and they didn't really know the government process very well. But they could probably do the work with luck and long hours.

"What if we get more than one of these jobs?" her finance officer asked.

"We'll worry about that when the time comes," Linda said.

Opportunities and Pitfalls

These three scenarios illustrate some of the most common opportunities and pitfalls of proposal writing. In the first scenario, the firm has targeted the right market and has the required skills and expertise. But the proposal-writing team is not experienced in responding to a high-level request. If the new hires don't learn in time, the company will lose out in the bidding war.

The second scenario represents a good match of company skills and client needs. Since many "green" firms are startups, their management is likely to make costly mistakes in marketing their services. However, Lee's firm is developing an unsolicited proposal. Their task is to convince clients that the firm's expertise and services can provide exactly what clients need. If the team does its homework, this firm has a good chance of creating a new client base.

The third scenario describes one of the most tempting pitfalls that new and even experienced companies encounter: shoot at every target in sight and hope you hit at least one. Valdez has made little effort to match client needs with her company's services and skills.

Even if a proposal is accepted, she has no way to assure the client that her firm can do the job within the proposed time and budget. If her firm has more than one proposal accepted, Valdez may not have enough staff to do any job well. At the very least, her company will waste a lot of time, money, and effort writing proposals for jobs they have little chance of winning or of completing to the client's satisfaction.

Types of Proposals

A proposal is primarily a sophisticated sales and marketing piece you develop to define a client's problem and/or opportunities and to sell the client on your ability to provide solutions and strategies to their satisfaction. To begin, let's look at the types of proposals you or your company may write. Proposals generally fall into four categories: internal, solicited, unsolicited, and sole-source.

Internal Proposals

Internal proposals are written within a company by a particular division, department, group, or individual to persuade top management to support an idea or project. For example, the product line manager may write a proposal to automate a particular assembly process. Even though these proposals are for internal consumption only, they follow the same principles as proposals written for outside companies or agencies.

Solicited Proposals

Sometimes, a company is formally invited to submit a proposal. They receive a request for proposal (RFP), request for quotation (RFQ), or bid invitation. The client has a particular project or problem and is looking for outside help to get the job done. The RFP or bid invitation outlines the requirements and criteria for the job. The client selects a supplier on the basis of a firm's recommended program, qualifications, and projected costs.

Unsolicited Proposals

Unsolicited proposals are the most risky to write. They may require considerable time and effort to develop with no guarantee that a client will be interested in the product or service offered. For example, a firm may develop a new program or concept, such as a new accounting method, and then must persuade clients to contract for the service.

Because the client has not requested the proposal, the firm must compete with a client's internal operations and other businesses for the client's attention and acceptance. On the other hand, these proposals are a way to generate new business for a company. As a rule, however, companies do not write unsolicited proposals unless they have solid reasons to believe they can win the client's business.

Sole-Source Contracts

In some instances, a government agency, private firm, or association will contract with only one company to supply a product or service. This practice is known as a sole-source contract and is generally established when a company has an outstanding record of reliability and performance. Such a company might submit a proposal for a sole-source contract not to compete for a job but simply to comply with regulations. The format is often standardized and requires detailed information about the product, delivery schedules, and pricing.

Your marketing research should be able to tell you when a supposedly open contract RFP is actually "wired," or targeted, for a specific company. This means that your firm has little or no chance of winning the contract, and you would be wise not to submit a proposal.

Request for Information and Request for Quote

There are a couple of variations of a formal RFP that you might want to consider answering. At times a client may send out a request for information (RFI) or a request for quote (RFQ).

RFI.
A client may start the RFP process with a request for information. Basically, the client wants to find out:

- Whether the requirements for a job they need to have done are reasonable.

- Whether the appropriate technology for the job exists.
- Whether solutions the client is considering are realistic.
- Whether you and other firms can meet the requirements of the job.

The client may ask you to point out potential problems, evaluate the available technology, and critique the client's project goals, schedules, and cost estimates. Because an RFI often leads to an RFP, you should consider responding to the client's inquiry. In many cases, the document you develop for the RFI can serve as your core materials for the RFP.

RFQ.

In a request for quote, the client provides more detailed requirements than those found in an RFP and may even specify how those requirements are to be met. You would be asked to supply specific quotes for each part of the work—including staffing, benchmarks, and a detailed breakdown of projected hours and costs. Like an RFP, a written RFQ is considered binding on your firm, unless the client's requirements change.

Exhibit 1.1 summarizes these four types of proposals and their characteristics.

Four Key Questions

When it comes to developing winning proposals, it doesn't matter whether your company is a Fortune 500 firm or the newest venture on the block. You still need to answer four basic questions:

- How do you set up your planning process?
- How do you elicit requests for proposals (RFPs) or locate job opportunities?
- How do you choose which jobs your firm should target?
- How do you write a winning proposal?

Your Planning Process

It may come as a surprise that the key to eliciting RFPs or locating job opportunities is not to hire a professional proposal writer but first to develop your company planning process. Without your

EXHIBIT 1.1

Proposals and Their Characteristics

Internal Proposals

Proposal written within a company by a particular division, department, group, or individual in the firm; it may be solicited or unsolicited.
- *Advantages*—those preparing the proposal know the firm's needs and the management structure; communication may be easier and decisions made more quickly than with outside clients.
- *Disadvantages*—the proposal must compete for scarce resources with other company business; if the proposal loses its management champion, the project may be canceled.

Solicited Proposal

Proposal written in response to an RFP from a potential client.
- *Advantages*—client is requesting a proposal, and the firm can select which RFPs to answer based on resources, expertise, previous experience, and time/cost calculations.
- *Disadvantages*—if the firm's bid/no-bid decision-making process is flawed, the firm may expend valuable resources researching, writing, and presenting the proposal with little chance of winning the job.

Unsolicited Proposal

Proposal that a company initiates without an RFP and sends to potential clients in an effort to obtain new business.
- *Advantages*—the firm can introduce itself to a wide range of companies; the same proposal can be sent to many firms, thus conserving company resources.
- *Disadvantages*—proposals are not tailored to individual companies; the firm may get more business than it can successfully handle.

Sole-Source Contracts

Primarily government projects that are tied to a specific firm; the RFP is sent not to request a competitive bid but to elicit detailed information on the product or services to be supplied in order to satisfy government regulations.
- *Advantages*—the firm contracted to do the work knows when the work will be coming in and the specifications; no resources are required to win the contract.
- *Disadvantages*—an outside firm responding to the RFP has little or no chance of winning the contract away from the company currently doing the work. If the contract *is* awarded to the bidding firm, they may have to use the specifications and parameters of the prior contractor.

planning process firmly in place, you will find it hard to write winning proposals and follow through on them. The company planning process creates a hierarchy of plans:

- Company mission
- Company business plan
- Company marketing plan

Once your planning process is in place, you can revise, update, and change your plans to meet changes in the internal and external environments. The planning cycle gives your company the flexibility to meet client needs and to stay one step ahead of the competition.

Your Company Mission

The company mission defines what kind of firm you want the company to be, what business you are in, and what your broad-range goals are. If you define your mission too narrowly, it can restrict your firm's growth. If you define the mission too broadly, it can take the company in too many directions.

The role of the company mission is clear: Until you know what business you are in and what you want to achieve, you can't plan for the future.

Your Business Plan

The business plan is the master plan that serves as the basis for all other plans in the company. It is a written document—prepared by top management—that covers all aspects of your business. Developing the plan gives you a chance to identify your firm's problems, opportunities, strengths, and weaknesses. The resulting business plan contains the company mission statement, agreed-upon goals and strategies for the company, market forecasts, new product development, pro forma financial statements, and many other aspects of the business.

Your Marketing Plan

Once the company's mission statement and business plan are set, you need to develop the marketing plan, or strategy. This plan supports the objectives of the business plan and helps the company achieve its goals and increase its profitability.

In today's economy, a well-defined marketing plan can serve as a blueprint to guide your firm as you seek to make the most of new business opportunities. The marketing plan can help you zero in on a target market, or niche, that emphasizes your strengths and minimizes your weaknesses. For example, a computer manufacturer may find that its current target customers are switching from desktop to notebook computers. The marketing plan can help the company reposition itself either to switch to the notebook product line or to find new markets for the desktop models.

In effect, you develop a marketing plan to narrow the field of potential clients to those you can serve exceptionally well, thus cultivating a reputation as a problem-solving firm. This approach can increase your chances of success for any proposal you write.

With a marketing strategy, your emphasis changes from simply selling products or services to selling *service* to clients, a subtle but powerful shift in philosophy. This requires that you research your clients to discover what needs or problems they have that *you are uniquely qualified to help them fulfill or solve*, those jobs that no one else can do as well as you can. The approach changes from, "Here are the services and skills we provide," to, "Here are how our services and skills can help to solve *your* problems and assist *your* growth."

Finally, a marketing strategy helps you take a longer view of business cycles and enables you to develop contingency plans for anticipating and responding to change. In today's global economy, national and international competition both within an industry and between industries is going to get a lot tougher. Everything from political systems to workplace technology to personal skills is undergoing rapid, unprecedented change. To survive, companies must use their marketing strategies to spot the opportunities that change brings and to adapt quickly, imaginatively, and effectively to new circumstances.

Summary of the Planning Process

In summary, a mission statement, business plan, and marketing plan enable you to:

- Identify what kind of firm you want to have, the type of business you are in, and what your overall goals and objectives are.

- Define your company's main product lines.
- Identify the company's strengths and weaknesses.
- Identify market niches in which your firm has an advantage over the competition.
- Identify potential clients within those niches and how you can help solve those clients' problems.
- Develop contingency plans to anticipate and adapt to a rapidly changing marketplace.

It is well worth your time to learn the planning process for your firm, whether you are a one-person sole proprietorship or part of a multinational corporate team.

Locating New Business

Once your firm has a clear understanding of its target market, the next step is obtaining business—whether from previous clients or new clients. Firms have several sources of business leads, including government and private agencies/nonprofit groups, industry sources, networks, and even personal speaking engagements.

One word of caution: Because funding practices and policies change so rapidly in today's environment, specific names and addresses for sources become outdated almost as quickly as they are published. Be sure to obtain the latest information on federal, state, city, and private/nonprofit agency contracts and grants. And don't overlook the reference librarian in your local library. Libraries have access to hundreds of government and private-sector databases and may be able to help you focus your research and cut down on your search time.

Government and Private Agencies/Nonprofit Groups

Government agencies from the federal level to local city councils contract with outside suppliers for many of their services. The *Commerce Business Daily*, published by the U.S. Department of Commerce, provides information on federal procurement invitations, contract awards, and subcontracting leads. This publication is available in print form or on the Commerce Department's Web site.

Some major cities also have private or government grant centers that provide a wide range of information on municipal, corporate, and private/nonprofit agency grants and contracts. You might be able to find examples of new RFPs and older proposals that were submitted, especially when it comes to government contracts. The Donors' Forum in Chicago, Illinois, is a good example of this type of resource. The U.S. Small Business Administration also has several hundred small business development centers across the country.

Many universities cooperate with state and federal governments to create small business incubators, which are resource groups that specialize in helping small businesses acquire information, technical resources, and funds. Again, you can conduct your own Web search or consult your local reference librarian to locate the names and addresses of these centers. Many of the centers' services are free to the public.

Industry Sources

There are several industry sources that can provide leads for potential clients and help you inform the market about your firm's services, products, and problem-solving skills.

Industry References.
Industry publications, associations, and funding centers list RFPs, contracts, and grants open for bidding. Such information is usually free to the public or can be obtained for a nominal fee or subscription rate.

Your Suppliers.
Many of your suppliers have connections with your potential clients. Suppliers often know of problems that a company is having and may pass that information on to you. Such tips could be the basis for an unsolicited RFP.

Personal Speaking Engagements.
Don't hesitate to sign up for a speaking engagement at an industry conference or trade group meeting. These engagements are great advertising for your firm and give you a forum for presenting your unique services and approaches to clients' problems. You can identify some of the major challenges facing businesses or problems within an industry. These events also are an opportunity for you to distribute brochures, client testimonials, and other printed materials

to audience members. Potential clients will have a chance to talk with you directly and ask questions about your firm.

An added bonus to these engagements is that you often get to hear, firsthand, what the competition has to say. If possible, try to get a list of all attendees at your event. This will provide you with contact information for potential clients.

Industry and Trade Shows.

Like speaking engagements, industry and trade shows are opportunities to tell potential clients who you are, what you do, and what results you've achieved for clients who have hired you. You want to get a booth in a high-traffic area or, if the show is particularly large, pay for two booths side by side. Make sure you have good displays and handouts, proper audio equipment, and your best speakers to talk with potential clients. One caution: remember not to give too many answers to people's more detailed questions about how you work. The person asking could be one of your competitors trying to get an advantage over you. Simply hand out your card and suggest that he or she call your office to set up a meeting to discuss things further.

Networks

The sources listed above represent the formal method of finding new business. Networks—your personal contacts with individuals working in industry, government, and private offices and agencies—represent informal and often far more effective sources of new business leads. In this highly wired electronic age, there are more ways than ever to keep in touch with your networks.

Networks can be built through contacts with people in industry associations; through client contacts and referrals; through volunteer work you do for various industry, government, and nonprofit agencies; and through personal friendships and professional relationships. People in your network will often supply essential background information on contracts and grants that can make the difference between winning or losing a job.

Your network contacts can keep you abreast of new contracts or grants coming up that may be suited to your firm. This advance warning can give you a jump on the competition. By the time the RFP or grant guidelines are published, you will be well into your research and writing phases of the proposal process.

Getting the inside story on contracts and grants can be an invaluable asset for your firm. Make sure that you give top priority to cultivating and maintaining your networks, particularly in today's environment, where more firms are going after fewer dollars.

Which Jobs to Target

Although it may seem like a good strategy to go after all the job prospects that you have even a remote chance of winning, actually the opposite is true. The more accurately you target specific projects that match your firm's capabilities, the more successful you are likely to be. It is important to satisfy your clients' needs, because your business depends on good referrals and recommendations from previous clients. Again, this is where a sound marketing plan can keep you focused on your target niche and prevent you from going in too many directions or chasing jobs that are only remotely related to your principal line of business.

But how do you decide which jobs your firm will pursue? This important preliminary process starts with top management, whether a corporate hierarchy or the one person who owns the entire business.

Management Responsibility

One of your first steps will be to develop a decision-making process that goes into action the moment an RFP or new business opportunity arrives. This process can be part of your firm's standard operating procedure for writing proposals. Key elements of the process should include the following:

- As soon as an RFP or other bid opportunity comes into the office, it must be reported to the person responsible for that area. The individual may be a vice president, contracts officer, or program manager. This policy ensures that no one sits on an RFP or contract bid and loses valuable time.
- Management should call a bid-decision meeting to assess whether a proposal should be written. If management decides that the company has a realistic chance of winning the job, a proposal should be prepared.
- Proposals should be assigned to those staff members most qualified to address the clients' concerns. Managers must

ensure that these staff members have enough time to do the job well and are not forced to develop the proposal on the side.

- If a team is assembled to write the proposal, they should have a specified area in which to work and be free from distractions or interruptions.

Bid-Decision Criteria

At the bid-decision meeting, assess each RFP or new opportunity in light of the following criteria:

1. *First and most important, does the proposal support your business and marketing plans?* The bids you decide to pursue should be in line with your mission statement and primary marketing goals. For example, if the goal of your firm is to increase business in city traffic planning contracts, an RFP from a health-care firm will pull you off your main objective. Make sure that the jobs you pursue support your business plan and marketing strategy.

2. *Does this project fall into your organization's area of expertise?* For example, if the RFP deals with upgrading cable relays and you are only beginning to venture into this area, do you have sufficient skills and resources to handle the job? Nothing kills a company's reputation faster than failure to perform the required work. Make sure you have the capability to follow through on the job. Otherwise, it's best to decline an RFP rather than risk compromising your firm's reputation.

3. *Does your background research on the project point out where your firm has a competitive edge over other companies?* Do you have more experience in this area? Is your staff better trained or educated? Can you come up with more innovative solutions to the clients' problems? You need to identify your major strengths and weaknesses *as they apply to this contract*, not your overall strengths and weaknesses. If you can't identify a clear competitive advantage for your firm, it may be better to decline the RFP and wait for the next opportunity.

4. *Have you worked for the client before or had significant contact with the client on other jobs?* If so, you often have a unique vantage point regarding their operations and problems. This fact can help give you a competitive edge over other firms.

5. *Can you assemble a proposal team and provide them with enough support and dedicated time to get the job done?* If your team does not have enough time or management support to write the best proposal, you decrease your chances of winning the contract.

6. *Finally, taking all other criteria into consideration, is there a realistic chance that your firm will receive the contract?* If your research shows that you have anything less than a 50 to 60 percent chance of winning a job, it is generally not worth your time to pursue it. Some experts say that a firm should not pursue any job unless they have an 80 percent or better chance of winning the contract. Also, see if you can determine whether another firm has been unofficially selected, or "wired," to get the contract or job. Your personal network contacts should be able to give you this information.

When *Not* to Write a Proposal

Your experience in your field and your knowledge of the competition should give you a good gut feeling about the chances of winning a contract. But it's always good to have a checklist for making a no-bid decision.

If any one or more of the following criteria hold true, you should seriously consider declining the RFP or job opportunity. Chances are that the solicitation has been made simply to satisfy regulations or to comply with federal or state laws.

- The time frame for preparing and submitting a proposal is completely unrealistic for you to do a good job.
- The RFP states that the current project is follow-up work for a multiple-stage project. You would be competing against the firm that completed the first part of the project. (However, it may be possible to subcontract with the original firm to do a portion of the work.)
- The technical or other specifications of the project do not match your systems but do match those of your competitors.
- The contract does not support your marketing plan or is out of your field of expertise.
- You have no real competitive edge over other firms.

- You do not have the staff or resources to prepare the best proposal your company can present.
- Your chances of winning the proposal are less than 50 percent or, as some experts advocate, less than 80 percent.

Sometimes your best decision can be to turn down an RFP. However, always maintain good relations with the client company. Write a letter thanking them for the opportunity to bid on the RFP, and then explain that you are declining the bid and why. Ask the company to include you on their list for future RFPs.

Characteristics of a Winning Proposal

If the RFP or new opportunity meets the bid-decision criteria, your task now shifts from deciding, "Should we do this proposal?" to, "How do we write a winning proposal?" Whether you are responding to an RFP or initiating the proposal, remember that your overriding purpose is to convince the client that *your firm is uniquely qualified to do the job.*

From the client's perspective, proposals make it possible to evaluate the skills and capabilities of a select range of companies and to choose the best firm for the job.

No matter who the prospective client may be and what problems must be solved, a winning proposal will always include at least the following elements:

1. *Evidence that you clearly understand the client's problem and situation.* It is astonishing how many proposals show that the submitting firm has *not* taken the time to research the client's problem and to state it clearly. Do background research to find out what the client truly needs. You may discover that the real problem is not what the client has stated in the RFP. This element is so important that it should be first on the proposal team's list and be featured prominently in the proposal document.
2. *A strategy and program plan or design that the client feels will solve the problem and produce the desired results.* The strategy and program plan is the heart of your proposal. The plan describes how you are going to solve clients' problems and

meet their needs. You should clearly state what benefits clients will gain by accepting your solutions. The proposal must tell clients enough without telling them everything. Otherwise, they may use your proposal to do the job themselves!

3. *Clear documentation of your firm's qualifications and capabilities for carrying out the program plan.* The client must be convinced that your firm has the required expertise and staff to accomplish the work better than anyone else. This documentation can take the form of a list of previous client work and résumés of staff members.

4. *Evidence that your firm is reliable and dependable. You can include references or client contacts who will vouch for your firm.* The new client must have confidence that you will deliver on your promises and will complete the job within the time and cost estimates you have developed.

5. *A convincing reason why the client should choose your firm over all the other firms competing for the job.* Do you have a better program plan, more expertise in the field, better staff, or some other competitive edge? Highlight this advantage; clients should feel they can't afford to do without you.

6. *Finally, your proposal should look like a winner.* Whether you submit a hard copy or an electronic version of your proposal, the cover, title page, format, and graphics should convey the spirit and professionalism of your company. Take the time to proofread your copy—do *not* rely on spell-check programs.

In the chapters that follow, you will learn how to develop a winning proposal, step by step—from the initial analysis of a client's situation, to the development of a program strategy, to the production of the final written proposal. Once you establish a proposal-writing process for your firm, you increase your chances of winning the contracts you pursue. And in today's business environment, you need every competitive advantage you can get.

2

9-Step Proposal Process: An Overview

Nicolle Herras selected a preliminary proposal team and called them together to discuss Everett Hospital's RFP. According to the RFP, Everett needed an interpreter network that would allow them to link translators with patients and hospital staff to improve patient care and staff effectiveness.

The IT manager spoke up. "Sounds like they need our collaborative care system. We could adapt the system to provide real-time voice/video linkups between off-site interpreters and the hospital staff."

Ms. Herras nodded. "That's a good start. What does everybody else think?"

The systems manager shook his head. "We have the system, all right, but it says in the RFP that the hospital is having trouble finding interpreters for some of the languages and having interpreters available 24/7. Are they expecting us to come up with a solution for that problem as well?"

One of the new hires, James Mullen, said, "A friend of mine works in a hospital in California, and they use a company called World Medical Interpreters. Maybe we could do a partnership arrangement with that organization."

Ms. Herras jotted down a note. "Mr. Mullen, you have that job—find out all you can about this company. All right, everybody, let's get to work researching the system requirements that might solve Everett's problems. Mr. Mullen, I'd like to talk with you and Laura Chiang for a moment."

After the others had left, Ms. Herras found the two new hires looking at her expectantly.

"I want you two to go over this RFP and find out what the client *really* needs besides what they've stated in the RFP. We need to make sure our system addresses all the key issues of this project. When the time comes, I want the two of you to collect the documents that our IT and systems departments will generate and put together the preliminary proposal."

James and Laura glanced at each other, and Laura voiced what seemed to be the feeling shared between them. "Ms. Herras, we appreciate your confidence in us, but to be honest, we're not first-rate writers, I mean, we can put together a decent section ..."

"Don't worry. I'll assign two writers to work with you on this. I'm more concerned about the client's real needs and our program design. You'll have all the support you need to help us develop a winning proposal."

*   *   *

Many people make the mistake of believing that the most important consideration in preparing a proposal is how well it is written or how professional it looks. Although good writing and a polished format are important ingredients, the most essential quality of a winning proposal is that it speaks to the client's real needs and sells the client on your company. In some cases, your research may reveal that the real issue is not what is stated in the RFP. You will have to deal with those expectations while gently leading the client to the topic you want to discuss.

For example, a chain of hardware stores losing business to a rival may believe that the problem is its stores' locations, product lines, demographics, or other factors. In contrast, your research may show that the real problem is lack of customer service—people are switching to the rival chain simply because they experience a higher level of customer satisfaction when they shop there. The rival company's sales staff is courteous and knowledgeable, customer orders are filled promptly, merchandise is guaranteed and, if not satisfactory, replaced or the customer's money refunded. The management is responsive to customer comments and complaints.

Your response to the RFP is to persuade the client tactfully that the real problem is poor customer service. You might say something like the following: "For chain stores, individual store location is often a factor contributing to declining sales. However, industry studies show that two other factors, product quality and customer service, also can seriously affect company revenue. Our initial review of your current situation does not indicate that store location or product quality is the major problem. We propose a broader study that would address customer service as a possible cause of your declining sales." Propose alternative approaches to address the problem and to achieve their goals: "By looking at customer service levels, we can determine what percentage of the decline in sales can be attributed to this problem. We can then devise strategies to correct the situation and to increase sales."

Keep in mind that however you might disagree with what the client believes the problems to be, you must answer those problems in your proposal. Otherwise, it will appear to the client that you have missed the critical issue in the RFP.

The major skills you need to create winning proposals are:

- Marketing and sales expertise
- Creative and analytical abilities
- Decision-making skills
- Interpretive skills

- Expertise in various subject areas
- Communication expertise (writing, client contact, presentation)
- Interpersonal skills

In this chapter, we provide an overview of the proposal preparation steps and look at how the required skills are applied. The ability to analyze an RFP and devote the necessary time and expertise to prepare a proposal should become a routine part of your company's operations. The preparation process can streamline your efforts each time you receive an RFP or when you want to make an unsolicited bid for a job.

9-Step Proposal Preparation and Writing Process

Whether you prepare an unsolicited proposal or respond to an RFP, the proposal preparation and writing process is fundamentally the same. It can be broken down into nine steps (summarized in Exhibit 2.1):

1. Conduct a bid/no-bid analysis and make a decision.
2. Assign an individual (or a leader and team) responsibility for proposal development. At this point, someone from upper management should be designated as the main client contact throughout the proposal process.
3. Analyze the RFP and develop a checklist. Also develop a preliminary unique selling point (USP) to address the issues in the RFP.
4. Develop a schedule for proposal preparation.
5. Assign and complete research, analysis, program development, and time/cost tasks.
6. Write a first draft and develop graphics.
7. Review and revise successive drafts.
8. Obtain final management approval of the proposal, prepare a cover letter or letter of transmittal, executive summary, appendixes or attachments, and other details.
9. Present the proposal to the client. If the proposal is not accepted, assign your firm's client contact to find out why the client chose a competitor's bid.

EXHIBIT 2.1

9-Step Proposal Preparation Process

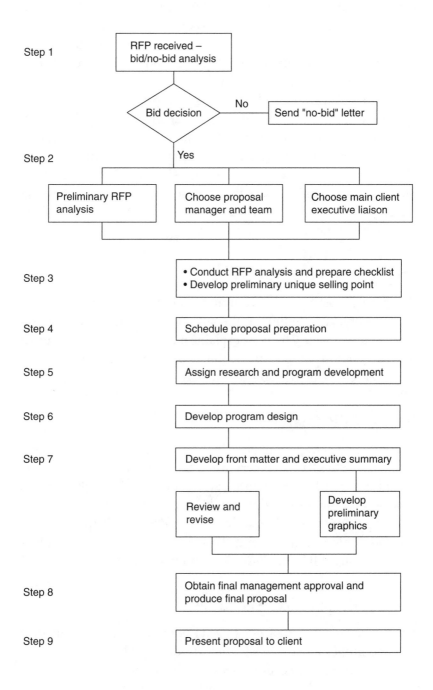

Step 1: Bid/No-Bid Analysis and Decision

The most important management decision a company makes regarding any given project is whether to bid for the contract. A proposal represents a significant investment of company resources and should be undertaken only if there is a reasonable chance of winning the contract. Or you may decide to accept a loss on the job if you wish to establish your company with a client, particularly if the prestige of the client will encourage other clients to hire your company.

There are two parts to this step: an analysis of the RFP and an economic analysis to determine whether the potential return outweighs the cost of preparing the proposal and completing the work. Chapter 3 describes the bid/no-bid analysis in detail and shows you how to decline a bid in a way that may generate future business. At the end of this chapter, we have included a list of sources and databases for conducting market research.

Step 2: The Proposal Team

The proposal team may be composed of only one person or several dozen people, depending on the size of your firm and the importance of the project. Chapter 3 explains how to build a good proposal team and outlines the responsibilities of each team member from manager to consultants to support staff.

Step 3: RFP Analysis

One of the most important tasks in the proposal preparation process is to analyze the RFP to determine what the client may really need in addition to what is stated in the document. This will help you develop your unique selling point that can make your firm stand out from the competition. Step 3 is covered in detail in Chapter 4: Finding Your Unique Selling Point. The work done in this step enables you to construct the proposal preparation schedule in Step 4.

Step 4: Preparation Schedule

One of the proposal manager's most important jobs is making sure that the proposal team meets their deadlines. The manager must plan the effort just like any other company project.

Exhibit 2.2 presents an example of a simplified schedule that can be adapted for most proposal preparation efforts.

Step 5: Assignment of Tasks

The preparation schedule allows the project manager to assign tasks and keep track of the individual (or group and coordinator) responsible for completing the task, key dates that work is due, and actual

EXHIBIT 2.2

Proposal Preparation Schedule

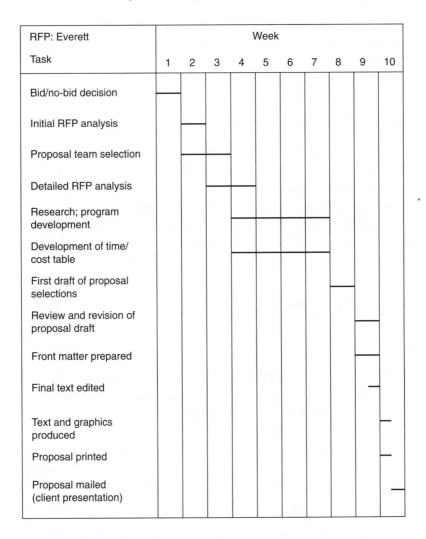

dates when the work is received. A more sophisticated method of assigning and tracking tasks is through the use of PERT/CPM (Program Evaluation and Review Technique with Critical Path Method) charts. These charts outline the critical steps in the proposal process, which are supported by less critical tasks, and assign a time frame to each step and task.

The preparation schedule with its assigned tasks and due dates tells the proposal manager quickly whether any part of the team is falling behind schedule or running into difficulties. The manager can then call in additional staff or resources to handle the situation. This "early warning system" can prevent every manager's nightmare of discovering two weeks before the first draft is due that a major section of the proposal is stalled. Such mistakes not only cost your company time and money, they may also cost your firm the contract.

Steps 4 and 5 are covered in more detail in Chapter 4: Finding Your Unique Selling Point.

Step 6: Development of Program Design

In Step 6, the proposal manager coordinates all information to develop the final program design. In this step, your firm pinpoints exactly what you will do for the client, how you will do it, and how much time and money it will take to finish the project. This step includes developing time and cost estimates. The program design is the heart of the proposal and is covered in more detail in Chapter 5: Developing Your Program Design.

Step 7: Development of Front Matter and Executive Summary

Once the first draft of the proposal is complete, top management will review it and usually suggest changes. When managers approve the final content, the proposal team will develop the front matter. This step is covered in detail in Chapter 6: Writing the Front Matter and Executive Summary.

Front matter for the proposal includes the cover (or transmittal) letter, final table of contents, list of any graphics and tables, and the executive summary. The executive summary is a key part of the proposal because it briefly describes the major issues and your firm's recommended actions. The executive summary serves as a potent sales and marketing piece for your company.

Step 8: Producing the Proposal

In Step 8, the manager gathers all proposal sections into one complete document, along with any graphics required. (Proposal production is covered in Chapter 7: Producing Your Proposal.) The proposal usually follows a set format, generally developed by each company. For example, many proposals have a format such as:

Title page
Cover letter or letter of transmittal
Table of contents
List of graphics and tables
Executive summary (summarizes main points and recommendations)

I. Statement of the client's problem (an analysis of the client's situation)

II. Program design (your proposed solution)
  A. Technical section (technical aspects of the program design)
  B. Management section (description of how the project will be managed and who will make up the management team)
  C. Time/cost section (estimates of time and cost necessary to complete the project, including follow-up)

III. Bidder's experience and qualifications (why your firm should be hired to do the work; this section can include an analysis of your competitors)

IV. Conclusions (your final opportunity to sell your proposal to the client, including a restatement of your solution and unique selling point, and how both will benefit the client)

V. Appendixes (staff résumés, recommendations from former clients, studies, surveys, contracts, other additional information not included in the text)

As you write, be sure that the reading level is appropriate to the client audience—neither too technical nor too simplistic. Keep formulas and equations to a minimum (unless they are part of the program design required to sell the proposal).

Once the first draft is completed, the review and revision process begins. Generally, top management will review the draft, often several times, and make suggestions or corrections. Your proposal team is responsible for incorporating these changes into the proposal.

The client may also review a draft of the proposal, depending on the situation. At this point, top management is likely to be in close contact with the managers of the client company. Although management changes may seem arbitrary at times, they are usually based on responses to client concerns or issues that come up in discussions with client management.

Step 8 includes production of the text and graphics. Chapter 7 offers guidelines on choosing the right graphics to present your data. As you produce your final proposal, resist the temptation to take shortcuts on quality control just to finish the work. One company took shortcuts and presented a flashy proposal to a client only to discover that the client's name had been misspelled on several key charts. Such simple mistakes can damage your credibility and make your competition look good.

Step 9: Client Presentation

Chapter 8 presents strategies for putting together winning client presentations. After all the hard work you have put into your proposal, you don't want to lose out on the final leg by failing to do a quality presentation. Your proposal deserves the best chance for success.

In some cases, you will simply deliver your finished proposal to the client and then spend a few nerve-wracking days, weeks, or even months waiting for an answer. If you win the contract, pop the champagne corks and start to work—your proposal effort has been successful.

In other cases, however, writing the proposal is only half the battle. You must also do a client presentation. Here is where your background research on client management and your face-to-face contacts with the client will prove invaluable. You need to know not only how to do a quality presentation but also how to anticipate who is likely to give you trouble and how to disarm their objections and soothe their fears. Make no mistake about it—for many managers and workers in the client company, you represent the often unwelcome prospect of change. This is particularly the case if people believe that their jobs may be in jeopardy or that they will be required to learn new procedures.

The chapters that follow discuss each of the nine steps in more detail. Chapter 3 presents resources to help you find what you need to know quickly and efficiently. Often, the key to successful proposal preparation is being able to locate the right information at the right time.

3

Selecting the Bid and Choosing the Proposal Team

Later that week, Ms. Herras met with her boss, Mr. Tagore, to discuss the Everett Hospital bid and to select the final proposal team. Mr. Tagore showed her the bid/no-bid analysis data for Everett and for a second RFP sent by another firm, Blue Ridge Health Services, Inc.

Mr. Tagore said, "We almost pursued the Blue Ridge RFP instead of the Everett RFP. Blue Ridge was a much bigger job with a lot more potential for follow-up projects."

Ms. Herras paused. "Really? I didn't know the race was that close. What tipped the balance in favor of Everett?"

"Two factors. Our preliminary background research showed that Blue Ridge has a history of loading extras onto the job and then refusing to pay the supplier any additional money. Second, I happen to know one of the execs at Goshen Consulting who did a job for Blue Ridge. She said that Goshen made only $10,000 on a $600,000 contract—all the changes and extra requirements ate up most of their profit."

Ms. Herras breathed a little easier. "So Everett is the better job all around."

"No question. According to the bid analysis, we not only have the resources and expertise for this job, but the return will be around 15 percent." Mr. Tagore glanced at her. "Unless you know of any other reason we shouldn't stick with this RFP."

Ms. Herras said, "There's only one issue we're looking into right now. We're not sure if Everett wants us to come up with a solution to their translator problem in addition to building a communication system. I've got the new hires, Mullen and Chiang, doing some background work on Everett, on medical interpreter providers, and on firms that are likely to be our strongest competitors. If we could get some kind of partnership arrangement with an interpreter provider for Everett, that could put us way out front in the running. We'd be offering Everett a complete package to solve their problems."

Mr. Tagore glanced at the proposal schedule. "You've got some tight deadlines here. Are you sure Mullen and Chiang can get all their work done in time?"

"They both have great research backgrounds. I'd be willing to bet that they finish their part of the proposal before anyone else does."

*   *   *

It is not uncommon for two or more RFPs to compete for your company's resources in the initial stages of the proposal process. On the surface, the jobs might look equally attractive. The bid/no-bid analysis can help you narrow the field to those jobs that are truly in your company's best interests to pursue. Once you have decided, you want to put together the best team to complete the research and writing stages in the most efficient, cost-effective manner possible.

This chapter offers guidelines on how to select or decline an RFP and how to choose an effective proposal team. You need to complete these steps before you go on to Step 3 (Chapter 4), in which you develop a detailed analysis of the RFP to determine the clients' needs and your unique selling point. At the end of this chapter, we also include a section on gathering market research and intelligence not only on the client but also on the industry and your major competitors. Collecting information for a successful proposal requires resourcefulness as well as research skills, but the effort can yield significant rewards if it gives your proposal a winning edge.

Step 1: Bid/No-Bid Analysis and Decision

As discussed in Chapter 1, conducting a bid/no-bid analysis and making a decision about a job will determine not only which bids you will pursue but also the business considerations that must be weighed for any potential job. In some cases, you may determine that the project may be only marginally profitable—or even represent a potential loss—but that the prestige of the client justifies bidding on the contract.

As listed in Chapter 1, the bid decision criteria are as follows:

1. Does the proposal support your total business and marketing goals?
2. Is the project within your firm's area of expertise?
3. Do you have a competitive edge over other firms?
4. Do you know the client from previous work?
5. Can you assemble and support an effective proposal team?
6. Do you have a realistic chance of winning the proposal?

The decision-making process is not limited to the initial bid/no-bid choice made when the RFP first arrives. Management also may have to decide whether to pursue the job at several points throughout the process, including after the proposal has been submitted. In one case, a firm submitted a bid to develop hardware for a cellular phone system, but, soon after, three key technical staff members left the firm to join a competitor overseas. With these key people gone, management decided to withdraw from the bidding.

Three Basic Cost Considerations

Before you start a more detailed analysis of an RFP, you need to consider three basic costs: financial cost, opportunity cost, and morale cost.

- *Financial cost:* This refers to the basic cost of researching, writing, and producing a proposal. How long do you estimate it will take you to accomplish this work? Would staff time and effort be used more effectively on another RFP or some other project? In other words, is the initial cost worth the potential return?
- *Opportunity cost:* You have only limited time in any given business year to go after projects. You can't afford to waste time responding to RFPs that are not right for your business. If you pursue a dubious RFP, you can't pursue other business that might bring you more success.
- *Morale cost:* Developing a proposal involves a high level of dedication and commitment from you and your staff. It's a blow to morale when all that effort results in the proposal losing out to the competition. By selecting opportunities carefully, you can increase your success rate and boost confidence and morale among your staff members.

Making the Bid/No-Bid Decision

The bid/no-bid analysis will not only prevent you from spending time and money pursuing jobs you have no chance of winning, but it will also keep you from winning jobs you can't perform.

There are several ways you can begin your bid/no-bid analysis of an RFP. One of the most practical and useful ways is to use a checklist, such as the one shown in Exhibit 3.1. You can adapt this sample checklist to fit your own company's requirements. A checklist can be useful not only for the analysis but also for developing the proposal, should you decide to pursue the job. It can help you:

- Identify the main points of the client's request and define their true needs.
- Discover items of concern and brainstorm strategies for the RFP.

- Reveal problems or opportunities that competitors might miss or ignore.
- Understand exactly what results or deliverables the client expects.
- Determine if the requirements are beyond the capabilities of your firm.

Keep in mind that you are responsible for living up to your contract, even if—through inexperience or lack of information—you underbid the cost or underestimate the time it will take to complete a project. Clients can take legal action to force completion of the contract or to obtain monetary damages for nonperformance. The damages can be considerable—even more than the dollar value of the contract. If you insist on taking such chances, make sure you have a good lawyer on retainer.

Once you have answered the basic questions on your checklist, or other method of preliminary analysis, you need to look at several issues more closely.

Organize the Information in an RFP and from Your Background Research.

In many cases, RFPs are written in logical order. Some, however, are so confusing and rambling that it's not clear what the client wants done or in what order. Make sure you list the client's requirements in an order that is clear and logical. For instance, a company should improve its inventory policies at the corporate level before trying to solve problems at a branch level.

The same requirement holds true of your background research. You may get conflicting information about a problem from different sources. If you put the information in a checklist according to data source—such as a database or personal interview—you can spot similarities among the sources. This step can ensure greater accuracy and confidence in your information.

Identify What the Learning Curve Might Be for This Project.

Are you going to have to invest a significant amount of time learning the client's business? If so, you may want to use the RFP as an opportunity to acquire new knowledge, skills, and experience. Many firms learn new industry sectors in this way. However, you will need

EXHIBIT 3.1

Checklist for RFP Bid/No-Bid Decision

RFP: Everett Hospital			Date Received: 9/16/20—
Criteria	Yes	No	Possible/ Unknown
RFP is a result of company campaign		✓	
RFP is an unexpected opportunity	✓		
Project supports our business/marketing goals	✓		
Project falls in our area of expertise	✓		
Client has stated needs or requirements clearly	✓		
Our strengths match the client's requirements	✓		
We have resources to fulfill work	✓		
We need extra resources to complete the work			✓
We can cover the costs of this proposal			
Client's payment and credit record is sound			
We can anticipate a return of at least XX% or more			
We have a competitive edge over other firms			
Project is part of multiproject work			
Project has potential for follow-up work			
Project will not affect other client relationships			
Project may represent conflict of interest with other clients or impair client relationships			
(Add more as needed.)			

to weigh potential benefits against the financial, opportunity, and morale costs for your firm.

Consider Your Firm's Reputation.

Have you positioned your firm as a key supplier of a product or service the RFP is requesting? You might want to go ahead with the RFP on that basis, unless there are clear circumstances that show you should decline it. Keep in mind, however, that declining the opportunity may do more damage to your reputation than submitting a proposal and losing.

Make Sure You Have a Unique Selling Point.

As you get further into your analysis, you should be able to identify the unique solution or product, known as a unique selling point or USP, your firm can offer the client. For example, everyone in the industry may offer voice-activated computers, but your firm can also provide voice-recognition passwords for parental control. With this advantage, you are in a good competitive position to win the project. Chapter 4 goes into more detail about developing your USP.

Decide Whether You Want to Bid Just to Stay on the List.

The RFP may be from a major client, an important prospect, or a government agency that you have been trying to break into. You may want to respond to the RFP simply to stay on the list and keep your firm's name in front of the decision makers.

Turning Down an RFP

At times, your analysis may lead to a no-bid decision. In this case, you can turn even a rejection of an RFP into a sales piece for your company if you take the time to do it properly. Do not simply throw the RFP away or fail to respond to the bid. Someone thought enough of your company to include you on the list. You can return the favor by being courteous enough to decline the job in writing. This strategy serves three purposes:

- It lets the bidder know you want to be considered for future jobs—or that you are not interested in future bids because the work is outside your area of expertise.
- It gives you a chance to highlight your company's strengths.

- It creates goodwill for your company. The bidder may pass your name on to other firms looking for bids on their work.

Generally, letters declining a bid are mailed about one week before the due date for submitting proposals. This gives you time to reconsider your decision should the client make any amendments or time extensions to the RFP.

Exhibit 3.2 provides an example of a letter declining an RFP. Notice that the format of the letter follows a specific pattern. First,

EXHIBIT 3.2
Sample Letter Declining an RFP

July 20, 20—

Ms. Ruth C. Nalamwar
Vice President of Operations
E-Tracer Telecommunications, Inc.
345 Rio Grande Boulevard
Cardiff, OR 87666

Dear Ms. Nalamwar:

Thank you for inviting us to submit a proposal for your rural relay project. The work will help connect remote mountain communities with important Internet and cell phone service providers.

We regret to inform you that Reardon and Associates will not be submitting a bid in response to your RFP #4421 titled, "Development of Rural Relay Systems in Skyler County, Oregon." Our expertise is primarily in fiber optical relays for underground cable systems. We have limited experience in the type of relay systems you wish to build in Skyler County.

Although we do not feel we can submit a superior proposal for this particular RFP, we would appreciate the opportunity to review other telecommunications projects in the future. Should you require any assistance in implementing the winning proposal, please do not hesitate to contact us. Our services may be useful for a more focused part of the project.

Sincerely,

Andre Brandon

Andre Brandon
President
(company name and contact information)

the writer thanks the client for asking the company to submit a proposal. Second, the writer states the main point of the letter by giving the reasons for declining the RFP. Finally, the writer finishes by highlighting the company's strengths and expressing a desire to receive other RFPs in the future.

Step 2: The Proposal Team

In some cases, only one individual needs to be assigned to prepare and write a proposal. But if the job is sizable or technically complex, you may need to pull together a team. There are four elements to a successful proposal team:

- *A manager to oversee the process.* This person is usually at the upper management level and may be a vice president or director of the firm.
- *Functional area managers, coordinators, or directors.* These people oversee the day-to-day work of the proposal-writing team. They are needed to coordinate such areas as background and marketing research, competitor information gathering, development of the program plan and budget, and identification of related company expertise and the résumés of staff members who will work on the project.
- *Team members with the requisite skills and knowledge.* These members come from all functional areas of the company and can include field representatives who often have special knowledge or insight into client needs. Members may also include outside consultants or companies that have specialized skills or knowledge regarding the RFP requirements.
- *Dedicated facilities for the team.* These can be as simple as a meeting room or as complex as a whole section of a company set aside for proposal work. A separate space allows the team to work more closely together and keep their computers, displays, and materials in one location.

The team structure might look like the one shown in Exhibit 3.3.

EXHIBIT 3.3

Sample of Team Structure

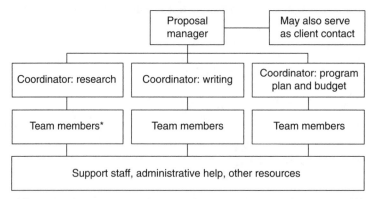

* Team members may come from teaming agreements or subcontracts with other firms as well as from in-house staff.

Proposal Manager

The proposal manager provides strong leadership and direction for the team. Even if this person is not an expert on the subject of the RFP, he or she should be knowledgeable enough to help direct and guide the efforts of the team. The individual should have some understanding of the company's IT capabilities and be able to motivate staff members and to coordinate and organize the work. It is essential that top management give the manager the necessary authority and support to see the job through to completion. Without top management backing, the proposal manager may not be able to obtain the necessary resources to do the best job. Finally, the manager must know how to set realistic goals to get a high-quality job done on time.

The manager's primary duties include:

- If assigned by the company, act as principal client contact and proposal manager.
- Recruit, organize, and direct the proposal planning team. This includes selecting coordinators to direct the activities of various groups involved in research, program development, time/cost analysis, and the like.
- Obtain the services of consultants and cooperating firms (if needed) and define their responsibilities and roles.

- Help the team analyze the RFP to determine the client's needs.
- Establish the proposal-planning schedule and assign tasks to individual members or team task groups.
- Ensure that the team stays on track and within established guidelines and goals.
- Review material submitted by team members.
- Maintain close contact with upper management to report on the team's progress and results and to obtain added assistance when and where it is required.
- Submit the draft proposal to top management.
- Assemble the final proposal and act as liaison between top management, client management, and the proposal team.
- Oversee production and delivery of the printed proposal and follow up to ensure that top management and the client received it.

The manager's primary job is to build the team and help them stay on target. He or she must encourage communication among members, foster mutual trust, and strengthen the team's commitment to achieve the goals of the proposal effort.

Functional Area Coordinators or Managers

The functional area managers, selected by the proposal manager, direct the efforts of their staff members and report to the proposal manager. This structure helps to build strong horizontal linkages between different departments or divisions of a company, which facilitates the proposal process. Generally, each group is responsible for developing and writing a section of the proposal. Coordinators make sure that each group's assigned tasks are completed on time. Their responsibilities include:

- Ensuring that the group understands the overall goals and purpose of the proposal.
- Preparing a detained outline of their proposal section.
- Assigning work tasks, setting page limits, and establishing work deadlines.
- Using consultants/subcontractors or cooperating organizations as required and integrating their input into the process.

- Reviewing drafts and participating in management reviews of draft material.
- Incorporating review comments into the final section copy and integrating this copy into the total proposal.
- Keeping the proposal manager apprised of the group's progress and requesting assistance as necessary.

Team Members

Team members generally are drawn from the ranks of company personnel and are chosen for the specific contributions they can make to proposal preparation. At times, outside consultants or companies may be required to complete the team roster. You can add outside staff either through consultant agreements or teaming agreements.

Consultant Agreements.

These agreements are made with individuals who have specialized, often highly technical, expertise. The agreement generally states the conditions under which the consultant will work with your company and contains a stipulation that he or she will not work for a competing firm during the terms of the agreement. If you win the contract and the consultant is to be included on the project team, this fact should also be stated in the proposal. The consultant's résumé should be included with other staff members.

It is important not to mislead the client regarding who will make up the staff. Some companies like to parade their experts in order to impress the client, particularly if they can drop the names of some "celebrity" consultants from the industry, academia, or technical fields. If the client awards your firm a contract on the basis of such name-dropping and later discovers that the consultant will not work on the project, the client might be justified in considering this action fraudulent and could cancel the contract or sue the firm.

Teaming Agreement.

A teaming agreement can be used to acquire expertise for the proposal preparation and/or to obtain an outside organization's capabilities to work on the project. This is known as a "go together and split" strategy. Two or more firms join forces to complete a project and then disband when it is over. In this case, the firms should choose only one person to act as principal liaison with the client. Otherwise, the risk of miscommunication between the client and the bidding firms is high.

Your firm may find it necessary to enter into teaming agreements with either two or three subcontractors to obtain all the talents and expertise the project may require. The client firm may look more favorably on this combined effort than they would on your firm's efforts alone.

The teaming agreement is a legal contract between your firm and the cooperating organizations. It establishes the conditions and restrictions under which the work will be done and defines the responsibilities of all parties. It is best if the legal staffs of all parties involved work out the details of the agreement to avoid future problems. As in the case of consultants, if cooperating organizations will also work on the client's project, this fact should be highlighted in the proposal.

Proposal Development Specialist

Some firms are turning to proposal development specialists to help them prepare proposals when the company has limited staff or funds to devote to a particular bid. The professional consultants serve either as proposal managers or as a one-person team coordinating proposal efforts. Some large organizations use teams of these specialists on a full-time basis to plan and develop proposals in various areas of client work.

Firms that do a considerable amount of business with the government, for example, may have proposal specialists who concentrate solely on preparing bids for different government agencies. Because complying with government bid specifications is so complex and is constantly changing, it often requires the full-time effort of a specialist. If your firm bids only occasionally on government projects, you should consider using an outside consulting firm to help you prepare the proposal. If the specialists act as proposal managers or coordinators, they will fulfill many of the same responsibilities as on-staff individuals.

Where to Look for Market Information

Market intelligence for proposals involves not only gathering information on the prospective client, the client's problems as stated in the RFP, and the environment in which they do business, but also on companies that may be bidding against you. In many instances you will have to do your research under tight deadlines, particularly if your company has delayed making a bid decision or has reversed a no-bid decision and is pursuing the job after all.

You can begin with basic sources of information to support your proposal writing. The major sources include:

- The client's RFP, staff, and other materials
- Your own company's knowledge, judgment, and experience
- Market and competitive analysis forms
- Your company's library, including swipe files (which contain studies, clippings, annual reports, past proposals, and other data that can be "swiped" for use in current proposals)
- Public information about the client
- Public and specialized databases
- Companies, associations, agencies, or groups specializing in marketing research and analysis

Often, the best place to begin gathering market intelligence is the client. At this point, it is important to have someone from your firm assigned to serve as the principal client contact. This person can go straight to the source and arrange for members of the proposal staff to interview client management and employees. An added bonus to this approach is that you may discover other dimensions to the problem that were not in the RFP or that the client has since uncovered.

The Client's RFP

It is well worth the time it takes to go over the client's RFP in detail. Even the most poorly written proposals, if studied carefully enough, will yield insights into the client's problems. This step will also help you guard against one of the most common—and potentially fatal— mistakes consultants and companies make: jumping to conclusions before they have a thorough understanding of the problem. This mistake will render your solutions meaningless and your entire proposal irrelevant.

Learn to read the RFP for what isn't expressly stated as well as for what is. For example, is the problem the result of a company's marketing approach or its marketing director? Is the client implying that there are political considerations behind the problem? Is there a deliberate gap in the information presented or a personal or corporate bias that may be coloring the situation?

Go over the RFP, using your checklist, until you are satisfied that you have gleaned everything you can from it and have identified the major areas that need to be researched. Not only will you have an in-depth understanding of what the client's problems are, but you will also have ideas about how to address them. In summary, read the RFP:

- For the basic facts regarding the client's situation
- To identify major research areas
- For what isn't said or what may be implied or suggested
- To avoid jumping to conclusions

Client Staff

Conversations with the client are often the second most important source of information after the RFP. If the bidding process permits, schedule talks with the client's management and staff. You may be able to record these conversations but, if not, be sure to take detailed notes. Memory is notoriously unreliable.

A note of caution: make sure you have done your homework and read carefully through the RFP before you talk with the client. Your questions should be designed to fill in gaps or obtain more detail on specific areas, not serve as a substitute for reading the RFP. You will not impress a busy executive by asking him or her to go over information that you should already know.

Try to talk with more than one level of management or staff. Very often upper management has only part of the picture, particularly where internal operations are concerned. Ask for a tour of the client's operations and branch office or plant sites. You may find that line workers or supervisors have more accurate knowledge of the cause and cure of many client problems. As more than one consulting company has discovered, a client may spend thousands of dollars for solutions that their own workers have already suggested but that management has discounted or rejected outright.

One major computer chip manufacturer, for example, hired a consulting company to find out why they were experiencing such a high rejection rate of components on the assembly line. The consultant in charge of the project discovered that every line worker knew the answer: faulty epoxy seals. The epoxy was not bonding to the silicon base. Line workers had reported the problem to management but had been ignored. As part of his report, the consultant recommended a system in which line worker suggestions were reviewed by a management board.

Tap the knowledge, experience, and judgment of client staff members to gain a fuller understanding of the client's situation and possible courses of action. The results of your research can be incorporated into your program design in the proposal. This step can help you tailor your proposal more closely to the needs of individual clients.

Client Materials

Client materials include annual reports, newsletters, brochures, position papers, articles published by company officials, press releases, consumer education pieces, and any other materials that help you understand the mission, products or services, and operating environment of the client. On the surface, these materials will tell you how clients perceive themselves—their corporate culture, position in their industry, relationships with their various markets—and will give you some idea of where they are heading.

To the practiced eye, however, these materials often reveal far more. Analyze them carefully with the following questions in mind:

- Are the materials conservative, daring, innovative, old-fashioned?
- What do the materials say about the financial health of the company and how the company is spending its money?
- Is the language focused on management achievements, the company as a whole, the consumer groups they seek to reach, or some other aspect of the business?
- Do they know their markets?
- Are they asking the right questions or offering the best solutions?

- Do they seem to be out of touch with their customers or with their own workforce?
- Is there a clash between what the materials say and how the company actually operates?
- Given their resources and potential, is the company aiming too high or too low?

The answers to these questions can give you key insights into the client's problems. For instance, one company made a point of announcing a new customer service package in its brochures, proudly pointing to a new toll-free number that would streamline the handling of customer concerns. In fact, when customers called the number, the line was always busy, making it difficult to get action on even minor complaints. Sales steadily declined over a six-month period. The company hired a consulting firm to correct the problem. The consultants analyzed the client materials, talked with consumers, and recommended a straightforward solution: the firm should deliver on the promises made in their brochures, which ultimately required adding a phone bank and more live operators.

Keep client materials on file in your databases. When you need to prepare a proposal, the materials will be readily available. A staff member can be assigned to update these materials on a regular basis.

Your Own Knowledge, Judgment, and Experience

As an outside consultant, one of the most valuable assets you have is the perspective you bring to a situation—a perspective that is almost always broader and more inclusive than any individual company possesses. You can draw on your years of experience in a variety of industries, markets and disciplines, or in one or two specific areas to help clients understand their problems in a new way. The market and competitive analysis form (Exhibit 4.6 in Chapter 4) will also be a source of valuable information in responding to an RFP.

Whenever you receive an RFP, try to see it in terms of the full range of clients you have served, rather than in light of only that particular client. Think about that client's management in terms of their background, culture, and style. Are there similarities to the management of other firms you know that might provide useful clues on how to approach the current client? Is the organization family-owned, for example? Or does the management emphasize team concepts, total quality management processes, or a more authoritarian approach? The answers to such questions will help you understand the firm's perspective on their own problems and what marketing approach might work best with this particular client.

Also determine whether there are solutions that worked in one discipline or field that might apply to the prospective client's situation. For example, could the queuing system you developed to manage a hospital's inventory apply to a retail chain's warehouse? Could the traffic pattern designed for a machine shop work in the greenhouses in a tree nursery?

Draw on the full resources of your company to encourage fresh, creative thinking on all RFPs you consider. This approach takes advantage of the horizontal links in your organization and throws the proposal review process wide open to innovative methods. In one firm, management regularly asked various departments to look over all RFPs and offer suggestions. In many instances, this apparently haphazard approach brought effective solutions more quickly and raised key questions much faster than if each department had worked in isolation.

Over the years, your company has developed considerable experience and judgment; put them to work for you on each RFP you receive.

Your Company's Proposal Databases

A well-stocked, well-maintained database can be as valuable to you as the fabled bank at Monte Carlo—and a lot more accessible. Your company should give top priority to updating and improving this data source to help you cut down on research time. Your proposal database should contain at least the following:

- Copies of previous proposals prepared by your firm
- Swipe files
- Competitors' proposals

Copies of Previous Proposals.
This resource comes under the heading of, "Why reinvent the wheel each time you need a wagon?" Keeping copies of proposals—

whether or not they were successful in winning contracts—can help the proposal team in several ways.

First, the successful proposals serve as models. The team can analyze why these proposals succeeded, how they were organized, and how they were presented. Second, all proposals are likely to contain valuable research and analysis that can save the team time and money. Third, proposals contain graphics, illustrations, tables, and appendixes that can serve as models for a current proposal.

Swipe Files.

Every company that regularly prepares responses to RFPs should have swipe files. These files include material from previous proposals, studies done on specific topics, information gleaned from newspapers and magazine articles and databases, informal or formal studies, "for your information" (FYI) items, and any other information deemed worth saving. Files are arranged by topic, company, industry, or other headings. Proposal researchers can access information through index terms or file headings and quickly find what they need. This technique is particularly valuable when time is of the essence and you need to pull information together on a variety of topics for a proposal.

Copies of Competitors' Proposals.

Try to obtain copies of your competitors' proposals, particularly those that won out over yours. If the bidding is open, you can ask the client for copies of competing proposals. At the least, try to find out from the client what key factors influenced the client's decision concerning who won or lost the bid. If you can obtain competitors' proposals, analyze them for information and insights into ways that you can improve your own proposals. The proposals may offer resources or studies that you may have missed in your own research.

It's often true that you learn more from your mistakes than from your successes. By obtaining copies of successful proposals from as many sources as possible, you increase your own chances of winning bids in the future.

Public Data Sources on Clients and Competitors

Another quick method of obtaining information on a client or competitor is to search public databases. This step is particularly valuable when the client or competitor is a well-established firm or organization. The more well-known public resources include:

- Dun & Bradstreet (D&B) reports. These give a brief description and a financial evaluation of the organization or firm.
- Directories such as a Standard & Poor's, Value Line, Thomas Register, Facts On File Directory of major public corporations, and Marketing Information Network. These directories give a description of the companies, their addresses and telephone numbers, earnings profiles, and names of key management personnel.
- References such as Business.com, Moody's Manuals online, Market Share Reporter, Business Rankings Annual, and *Competitive Intelligence Advantage* (published by John Wiley & Sons, 2009). Such references provide additional information on companies and may give you insights into their operations and current issues.
- Journals, periodicals, and online publications specializing in business reporting, particularly *The Wall Street Journal, Fortune, Investors' Business Daily, Forbes, Barron's, Bloomberg Businessweek,* and specialty publications for various industries. These sources provide up-to-date information on companies' current conditions and market environment.

In addition, small companies, sole proprietorships, and firms with limited budgets should not forget a resource found in many major cities: the public library. Reference librarians are trained in database research, and many libraries in major cities have special business research collections to serve the surrounding business community. A good research librarian can significantly reduce the time, effort, and cost it takes to track down information on a client.

Public and Specialized Databases

Public and specialized databases either cover general business information or serve the needs of a particular industry or profession such as banking and finance, health care, food service, government agencies, toxic waste disposal, engineering, and others.

General Databases.

Some of the more common databases used in business proposal research include:

- *Citibase (1947 to present):* Provides financial indicators for the U.S. economy, U.S./international transactions, population, employment, earnings, and more.
- *Citibase (weekly updates):* Provides weekly information on the U.S. economy.
- *Dialog Information Services:* A composite of several hundred databases providing information on various topics and industries, for example, APTIC (air pollution control), MEDLINE and meshline (medical topics), Psych Abstracts, and others.
- *Drug Information Fulltext:* Provides full text of hundreds of monographs covering more than 50,000 commercially available and experimental drugs in the United States.
- *Global Vantage, Ltd.:* Offers corporate financial data covering several thousand companies in the United States and other countries.
- *Toxnet:* United States National Library of Medicine Web site that offers information on several thousand hazardous substances.
- *Market Potential:* Offers demographics and U.S. population figures and marketing consumer surveys; provides a Market Potential index on a product or service.
- *Mergers & Acquisitions:* Provides corporate finance data for U.S. companies.
- *MortgageStats:* Offers information on U.S. securities.
- *U.S. Patent and Trademark Office:* Provides information on any patent registered with the U.S. Patent Office.

This is only a partial list of the many databases available to researchers.

Business and Professional Networks.

There seems to be a network on the Web for every type of profession and field. Only you and your firm can determine which ones are the most useful to you, since members tend to come and go. Some that seem to have endurance are networks such as LinkedIn.

These networks can provide invaluable contacts, resources, and leads for your company. Always verify any information gained through this type of source to ensure its accuracy.

Specialized Research and Information Groups

Information management firms help you find what you need from the avalanche of data that confronts you today. You can find these firms listed on the Web. They offer services that range from monitoring specific databases and highlighting information to preparing formal reports on requested topics.

When you are under a tight deadline to put a proposal together, it may be worth the money to hire one of these specialized research and information groups to do your background work or studies for you. You can then concentrate on developing the USP, program design, and recommendations sections of the proposal. In some cases, you may consider hiring staff from these groups as part of your proposal team. Such collaborative efforts can enhance your resources without taking away from your current staff.

Some firms hire these groups to do proactive research, that is, to gather information not currently needed but likely to prove valuable in the future. Such information can then be used in a proposal when needed.

Once you have decided to submit a proposal and have gathered your preliminary data, you're ready for the next steps. Step 3: detailed RFP analysis and your unique selling point, Step 4: preparing your proposal schedules, and Step 5: assigning team members specific tasks.

4

Finding Your Unique Selling Point

After the bid decision had been made, James Mullen and Laura Chiang met with Ms. Herras and the rest of the Integrated Medical Systems proposal team, which included staff from marketing, IT, and software departments. Ms. Herras also had opened the meeting to anyone in the company who wanted to sit in on the discussion. To start off, she asked James and Laura to share the results of their research.

James explained the background of Everett's RFP.

"Everett Hospital is the major health-care facility in its area, serving a rural community, several small towns, and two larger cities. Over the past couple of years, this area has experienced a big influx of refugees and immigrants from several Middle Eastern, African, and Asian countries. In fact, they deal with a diverse patient population that speaks over 60 different languages and dialects."

Sy Warner from the company's IT department interrupted. "Sounds like they need an efficient way to interface with outside interpreters."

Laura Chiang nodded. "When we went through the RFP, we found the terms "patient-clinician communication" and "better patient outcomes" about 25 times, so these are really high priorities for Everett. And they don't need interpreters just to give better care to their patients. Major care facilities are mandated by federal regulations to provide patients with translators in order to receive payment for federally funded programs. Everett already has voice and video hookups to consult with physicians around the world. What they need is an interactive voice/video network that gives them rapid access to outside interpreters."

James added, "It has to be voice/video, because hearing-impaired patients need sign language interpreters."

Ami Sarira from marketing chimed in. "What about links to diagnostic and lab data—should that be part of the system? And what about security? I'm sure they don't want any of their patient interviews to show up on YouTube."

James pointed to his laptop. "That's all part of the RFP requirements. But there are some gaps in the RFP. For instance, Everett didn't explicitly state that they wanted us to help them partner with an outside language interpreter service, but I don't see how they're going to solve their problems without it. World Medical Interpreters, Inc., is one service we're talking with about linking up with Everett. World Medical already has a broad network of medical interpreters in over 120 countries."

Carl Briech from software development spoke up. "I've been looking over this RFP, and I'm not sure exactly what they expect in terms of tech support, system maintenance, and in-service training of Everett's staff."

James nodded. "You're right. They were vague on that. We'll have to get more information from the client. Laura and I are generating a list of questions to ask them, so if anyone has questions they want answered, just shoot us an e-mail."

Trisha Opinsky from accounting raised another issue. "So who's our major competition for this job?"

Laura glanced at her laptop. "Four consulting firms, but only two really count: Tri-City Medical Consultants and SunWorks. They both offer systems similar to ours, and they've both worked for hospital or medical care facilities. We're going to have to work hard to beat them."

Sy Warner said, "I know SunWorks is developing a new video streaming package that's faster than ours. But I believe we still have the edge in definition and signal stability, and I *know* we have better security programs."

Ami Sarira had a sudden thought. "This new system would be great publicity for the hospital. We could work with their PR staff on how to publicize it to the community. It would also make a great community outreach story."

Ms. Herras had been jotting down notes during the meeting and now interrupted the discussion.

"All right, so far I think we've identified some key client needs, some of our gaps, and our major competition. It also looks like we've got our preliminary USP and client benefits. As I understand, Everett wants a consulting firm that will build them an interactive and secure voice/video system to provide rapid access to a wide range of interpreter services. If we can offer them both the system and connections to a pool of trained medical interpreters, we'll have a real edge over the competition. The benefits for Everett include greatly improved patient-clinician communication, reduction in medical errors, compliance with government regulations, elimination of a host of liabilities for the hospital, and better patient outcomes and postcare follow-up.

"Mullen and Chiang, keep working on your contacts with World Medical. All right, people, let's get on this. We've got three weeks to put this proposal together. I want to see the first draft of the program design one week from today. I'll work out the scheduling and assignment details for everyone. Personally, I think we have a great shot at winning this job."

*   *   *

Step 3: Detailed RFP Analysis and Your USP

When your initial analysis of the RFP and your background research are completed, you are ready to launch into the detailed RFP analysis to find your USP. The work in this chapter covers Step 3 (detailed

RFP analysis and USP), Step 4 (schedule preparation), and Step 5 (assignment of tasks in the proposal writing process). As the firm in the example above learned, part of your solution may be revealed by what *isn't* stated in the RFP. As we mentioned earlier, the gaps you uncover in your analysis can be as important in developing your solution as the information that is clearly stated in the RFP.

A detailed analysis of the RFP will help you formulate your USP, which shows the client how you stand out from the competition. In turn, your USP will drive the detailed plans for each part of the program design, as described in Chapter 5.

Three Purposes of the Analysis

The RFP analysis step serves three purposes:

- To define the problems and requirements you must address.
- To determine what resources and information you will need in order to write the proposal.
- To generate the specific tasks that the team groups will be assigned.

For this step, you may want to pull in staff members from several departments or areas to help analyze the RFP and develop the main elements of the USP. Often, throwing the process open to this kind of cross-fertilization can be highly effective.

RFP Analysis Checklist

You can create an RFP analysis checklist, similar to the bid/no-bid decision checklist in Chapter 3, to help you with this step. This checklist, such as the one illustrated in Exhibit 4.1, provides spaces to list the following information:

- Client's problem or requirement.
- RFP page number.
- Work your team needs to do regarding the problem or requirement.
- Who is assigned specific tasks.
- Date work is due and the date it is actually delivered.
- Page number of your final proposal that responds to the client's original problem or requirement.

EXHIBIT 4.1

Checklist for RFP Analysis and Task Assignment

RFP: 621–853—Everett Hospital							
Problem/RFP requirements	RFP page no.	Input/task assignment	Assigned to	Date due	Date received	Proposal program page no.	Comments
Supplying inter-preters for over 60 languages spoken at Everett	5	Talk with World Medical Interpreters about partnering agreement	Mullen and Chiang	10/15	10/17	8	WMI very receptive to partnering agreement

By glancing at the checklist, the proposal manager and the team member coordinators know exactly where they are in the development process.

This checklist can help you identify gaps in your knowledge or database. For example, an alternative energy firm may have perfected a new type of biofuel using algae by-products. However, if the public is leery of using the product, it will be a financial failure. The proposal researchers would need to learn more about this biofuel and then investigate the best way to persuade customers to accept it. The results of their research would be incorporated into the program design section of the proposal.

In addition, you can include an edited version of the checklist in your final proposal to give the client a "road map" showing your responses to each of the client's problems and requirements. In this way, you provide a concise summary of the selling points of your proposal. Of course, you should exclude the "comments" column before showing the checklist to the client.

Remember, you need to address all the elements listed in the RFP or you may lose out in the bidding competition. This is true even if you discover that some items the client has identified are not related to the actual problem. The client *believes* they are related, and you must discuss them. For example, a client may state that sales decline is the result of poor advertising campaigns, but the real reason is poor service. Still, you must tactfully cover the point the client raised. Your proposal might state it like this:

"Although advertising campaigns have an impact on sales, industry studies show that the effect is nearly always short term and does not account for a persistent decline or uneven pattern in sales. If product quality or customer service is poor, effective advertising will not offset consumers' negative perceptions of a company. In fact, an effective advertising campaign generally raises customers' expectations and decreases their tolerance for poor service or defective merchandise."

Once you have developed a checklist form, the RFP can be analyzed in two stages: an initial quick evaluation and a more detailed analysis.

Quick Evaluation

The initial evaluation can take as little as five or ten minutes to complete and is one way to obtain an overview of the client's requirements. Your cursory survey can tell you:

- The client's main problem or requirement.
- What special resources the client requires.
- What restrictions are placed on who may bid for the contract.
- How much time you have to complete the work.

This step can give you a rough idea of what the job entails and what resources you are likely to need. You will also be able to spot any major gaps in your knowledge or in your company's expertise and experience. You can then take steps to fill in the gaps, either through research or by using outside expertise.

Detailed Analysis: Key Questions

Your next step will be to prepare a detailed analysis of the RFP. Remember, your goal is to develop a proposal that is client-based, not one that merely showcases your firm's staff, expertise, and creative solutions. Always ask yourself: How will the client benefit from any solutions or recommendations we propose?

As you conduct your detailed analysis, you will need to answer such key questions as the following:

1. *What is the client's real versus stated problem?* Clients often confuse symptoms with underlying causes. For example, they may focus on a declining market share rather than on production problems. Or they may focus on worker morale rather than on their own management policies that may be causing a decline in morale. It is your job to identify the real problem or situation facing the client. Start with the client's view of the problem and then look deeper. This is where your background research into the client's history and performance will be invaluable.

2. *What does the client believe is the solution?* Clients frequently believe that they know the solution to their own problems. However, if they are not seeing the real issue, then their answers will also be faulty. For example, if the client believes that the problem is declining market share, they may feel that the answer is to increase advertising or develop a better promotional campaign. If the actual problem is product quality, more advertising is not the solution. You will have to listen to the client and persuade them that they will need to improve the quality of their product. This persuasive task must be done without offending client management (i.e., without implying that managers are incompetent, cut corners for profits, have no sense of the market, etc.). Always keep the focus on fixing the problem, not the blame.

3. *What experience do you have in handling the client's problem or requirements?* As you go through the RFP, noting problems and potential solutions, you should also be noting what expertise or experience you have to address the issues. You need to build solid trust and credibility with the client and show that you have the staff and track record to do the job. To improve production facilities, for example, you can note in the checklist which staff members in your company have production experience and where your gaps in knowledge or

experience lie. These gaps will have to be filled in before you submit your final proposal. In this way, you not only get a clear picture of your current resources but also of what resources your company needs for the future. This item can be seen as building a résumé for your company, highlighting your firm's previous experience in the client's field, your prior contracts, and the types of work you have successfully completed. Nothing inspires a client's trust and confidence in your abilities like success.

4. *Who are your main competitors?* Competitor analysis is a critical component of preparing a winning proposal and should be part of the team's assigned research tasks. You need to know who your competition is and what they are likely to offer. After each client problem or requirement in the RFP analysis checklist, note which competitor would be able to address that issue and what their solution might be. In the case of the client with production problems, for example, ask which competitor has production experts or experience in the client's line of business.

   Should the client ask you about the capabilities of a rival firm—as a client often will—you will not only be able to discuss that firm but to explain why your company can do a better job. Knowledge of one's competitors can make the difference between winning or losing a job.

The Market and Competitive Analysis Form at the end of this chapter can help you analyze your competition (see Exhibit 4.6 on pp. 73–76). You may want to customize the list of questions to meet your exact needs. This form provides you with information that will highlight the advantages you have over your competitors and help you pinpoint your competitors' weaknesses, gaps, and lack of resources. You may also uncover your own deficiencies, which will help you devise a strategy to minimize or compensate for them.

As you complete this form for different competitors, you are building a file on each company. You can also keep track of the competition's changing position in the marketplace. Is the competition filling in its gaps? In what direction is management taking the firm? Knowing the answers to these and other questions can help you stay ahead of the competition.

The Market and Competitive Analysis Form covers five major areas:

- Service offerings
- Company strengths and weaknesses
- Strategies
- Market shares
- Market segments

Fill out a form for each service or product your company may offer. Make sure that your department heads and other pertinent staff members receive a completed form and add their own comments. (If you need additional information on interpreting your results, see Hamper and Baugh, *Strategic Market Planning*, McGraw-Hill, 2000.)

5. *What is your USP likely to be?* At this point you should have an idea of what program or USP you have to offer the client. You may not know in detail, but you can list your ideas or insights on the checklist.

   For example, if the client's exporting process needs improvement, your USP may be a specific set of workflow steps to make the process more efficient. You may not know at this stage whether the process will work for the client, but it could be the edge you need. By jotting down your ideas or insights, you keep a record for further development and for future RFPs.

6. *What are the benefits of your USP to the client?* Always keep a list of the benefits that your USP provides to the client. Benefits to the client are a key component of a winning proposal. Many firms lose out in the bidding process because they focus mainly on what their company can provide and neglect to state what benefits the client will gain. For example, if you can increase the client's production efficiency by 10 percent, what does this mean? Will the client save a significant amount of money in production costs? Will they improve their per-unit profit margin? Will their products be more competitive in the market? Always spell out client benefits.

Your answers to questions 5 and 6 can serve as the basis for the first rough draft of the proposal. The next stage would then be a more complete draft that would be submitted to upper management for review. You will probably go through several drafts before producing the final version.

7. *Who will be on the project team?* One of the key preparation steps is selecting the right personnel to do the job for the client. At this stage, you can begin updating résumés of key staff members who are likely to form your project team. Résumés should be slanted toward the client's needs, highlighting your staff's experience, knowledge, or expertise in areas that address the client's problem or situation. See sample résumés in Appendix C.

8. *Will the preparation effort require any demonstrations, benchmark tests, or other preliminary work?* In some cases, the RFP will indicate a need for you to perform some type of demonstration or benchmark test to convince the client that your firm is capable of doing the work. For example, you may need to demonstrate how product quality has slipped or how the client's current time and expense accounting has become inefficient. Such demonstrations or tests will require time to develop. You will need to indicate on the checklist who will be assigned this task and the estimated time required.

    A word of caution: Make sure your demonstration or test focuses on defining and clarifying the problem *as the client perceives it* and not as you perceive it. Also, check to be doubly sure that the demonstration or test does not inadvertently tell the client how to solve the problem. Otherwise, you have just given away your solution for free.

9. *How much will the proposal effort cost your firm?* The time and staff costs of preparing proposals should be charged to a separate account. The estimates should include such items as writing, production, and printing expenses, as well as travel, staff salaries, and research costs. The easiest way to obtain a fairly accurate estimate is by starting with the expected value of the client contract and working backward.

10. *Who in the client's organization is likely to support or oppose your proposal?* The checklist can also help you note the political climate in a client's organization. What is the philosophy of top management? Who are the key decision makers? Are there any managers or executives who may argue against your firm? For example, if the client has quality control problems,

is the director of that department likely to support or resist proposed changes? The answers to these questions can help you overcome the objections of some managers or executives and ensure that your proposal has a greater chance of success.

These 10 basic questions will focus your detailed analysis and help you develop a client-oriented proposal. The more completely you understand the RFP from the client's point of view, the more likely your proposed solutions will match the client's needs.

Asking the Client for Information

In many cases, the RFP may not be clear about certain specifications or conditions, or there may be gaps in the RFP you need to fill. You can use the basic questions above as a starting point to generate more focused and detailed questions for the client.

Make sure you protect your own interests when asking for information. Find out from the client if all bidders will see one another's questions. If so, make sure you are not giving away proprietary information or tipping your hand to your competitors. If you have questions you'd like the client to answer that involve revealing a key piece of your solution or some other sensitive material, request a private meeting to discuss them. You can also ask the client to sign a proprietary or confidentiality agreement stating that no one in the company will reveal the content of your questions.

Once you have obtained the information you need, you can begin to focus on your solution and USP.

Customized Service and Value

When clients ask for proposals, they are looking for customized service tailored to their particular needs and goals, and they want the highest value for their money. The USP that you develop has to deliver not only in terms of performance but also in terms of this type of value.

Keep in mind that an *acceptable* proposal is not enough. Every one of your competitors is likely to turn in an acceptable proposal. A *winning* proposal must go one step further and do *all* of the following to provide the highest value for the client's dollar:

- Show a detailed, achievable plan clearly stating how you will solve the client's problem within the constraints of the RFP and what benefits the client will receive.
- Sell the client on the credibility of your plan and your firm. Your proposal must create absolute confidence that your firm can deliver the promised service or product.
- Meet all RFP requirements, including delivering the proposal to the client *before* the stated deadline.

The information from your background research will prove invaluable at this point. Remember, your background research should cover the following:

- The topic of the RFP, a brief background of the project, and the client's history, organization, and budget for the project.
- The competition's strengths and weaknesses compared with your firm's strengths and weaknesses regarding the RFP topic. For example, your competition may be strong in software programming in general, but less experienced in a specific type of software programming. This fact gives your firm an advantage that can be a selling point to the client.
- The target market for the RFP product. Your target market is basically the client organization, along with its constituents. In the sample case, for instance, Integrated Medical Systems' product includes (1) an interactive communications voice/video network with technical support and in-service training and (2) links with an outside medical interpreter service. Integrated Medical Systems' target market is Everett Hospital, specifically the health-care staff and the patient population that speaks over 60 different languages and dialects.

Client's Needs and Wants

Using this background research, the proposal team should be able to generate a prioritized list of the client's needs and wants. Exhibit 4.2, Client's Needs/Wants Analysis Form, will help you determine these needs/wants, your firm's response to each one, your competitor's likely response to each, and a comment section where you can interpret the responses. For Everett Hospital, Integrated Medical Systems' list might read as follows:

1. Assessment of Everett's current interpreter needs and of the most critical patient areas where services must be acquired rapidly.
2. Assessment of Everett's current interactive voice/video system hardware, software, and security.
3. Negotiation of potential agreement with outside interpreter service.
4. Design of new system to access off-site interpreter service with call manager to route requests for specific medical interpreters.
5. Design of wide area network to make new service available in all patient care areas and to access diagnostic and lab data on demand.
6. Assessment of tech support, maintenance, and in-service training required to maintain and upgrade the system.
7. Development of staff, time, and cost estimates to complete the work.

When filling out the form, be ruthlessly honest. For example, if you have problems with cost overruns or take longer to develop a product than your competitors, admit it. Only you and your staff will see the list, so there is no point in dodging the truth. If you cannot base your proposal on reality, you are better off not trying for the job.

Once all the responses have been interpreted, look at the form in its entirety and summarize its contents. This will enable you to develop a proposal that will address all the client's needs/wants, which will help give you an edge over your competitors.

After you have finished the form, take time to reanalyze what you believe your competitors' likely responses will be. The rationale for doing the analysis a second time is simple: some managers have a tendency to minimize their competitors' strengths and exaggerate their weaknesses to the point where the responses are distorted. Such a tendency will only reduce your chances of winning the bid. You may have to use your intuition on some of the items, but you probably know your competition better than you think you do.

EXHIBIT 4.2
Client Needs/Wants Analysis Form

Client: _____   Date:_____

Proposal Manager: _____

1) Client's need/want

Software program to format medical data to permit easy access, analysis, and transmission to computer systems of other drug treatment centers.

Our firm's response

_____

_____

_____

Competitor's likely response

_____

_____

_____

Comments

_____

_____

_____

2) Client's need/want

Extensive knowledge of drug treatment programs and their administrators and staff.

Our firm's response

_____

_____

_____

Competitor's likely response

_____

_____

_____

Comments

_____

_____

_____

3) Client's need/want

Software that will be easy to update, highly reliable, user-friendly, and adaptable to change in technology.

Our firm's response

_____

_____

_____

EXHIBIT 4.2 *(Continued)*

Competitor's likely response

_____

_____

_____

Comments

_____

_____

_____

4) Client's need/want
   Reasonable development time and cost.
   Our firm's response

_____

_____

   Competitor's likely response

_____

_____

   Comments

_____

_____

_____

5) Client's need/want
   Sales and marketing expertise to market product.
   Our firm's response

_____

_____

_____

   Competitor's likely response

_____

_____

_____

   Comments

_____

_____

_____

   Final summary

_____

_____

This form, when completed, will show you where you have a competitive advantage or disadvantage. The areas of clear advantage generally form the basis of your unique selling point and give you a list of client benefits. For Integrated Medical Systems, their USP advantage is twofold: (1) they can create a high-definition, stable, and secure voice/video network to help hospital staff access interpreters and patient data quickly, and (2) they can help Everett link with an outside service to find the medical interpreters that the facility needs.

Value-Added Elements

While developing your USP strategy, keep in mind that you may be able to add features as you go along. This value-added approach enables you to respond to information you gain from the client or from additional research. You might use a form to record your ideas, such as the one shown in Exhibit 4.3. For instance, Integrated Medical Systems' marketing strategy for Everett Hospital might include any or all of the following elements:

- Estimated reductions in health-care costs resulting from more efficient use of staff time and hospital facilities.
- Methods to quantify patient satisfaction and compliance with medical instructions.
- Methods to track the reduction of postoperative complications resulting from more effective patient-clinician communication.
- Suggested phased plan for Everett to install the same level of interpreter service in their satellite care facilities at an affordable cost.
- Education of Everett's PR staff members to help them publicize the new interpreter service to the community and to the media.

Each element should be considered part of the entire proposal strategy, much like modular units are part of a whole. This modular approach to building in value and value-added elements makes your solution more flexible and allows you to tailor it more precisely to the client's needs. For example, Integrated Medical Systems may be able to include some of the following value-added items to their proposal to highlight the company's unique strengths:

EXHIBIT 4.3

Value-Added Elements Form

Instructions:

1. Fill in the information at the top of the form: client, date, proposal manager, and names of your primary competitors in the bidding process.

2. After each element in the list, analyze your firm compared to your competitor(s). Use a "+" sign to indicate an advantage your firm possesses; a "o" when you and the competition are equal; and a "−" to indicate when your firm is at a disadvantage compared to the competitors. You can customize the list for your particular situation.

3. Use the comments section to note whether an element adds to the value of your plan, indicates a strength or weakness of your firm or your competitors, or reveals other information that may be useful in developing your unique selling point.

Value-Added Elements Form

Client: Everett Hospital   Date: 9/17/20—

Proposal Manager.: Ms. Herras

Element	Your firm	Competitor 1	Competitor 2	Comments
1. Service				
2. Training				
3. Technical support				
4. Software upgrades				
5. Geographic coverage				
6. Pricing				
7. Service line breadth				
8. Service differentiation				
9. Employees' backgrounds				
10. Service quality				
11. Compatibility				
12. Breadth of service application				

Comments summary

_____

_____

_____

- Provide different levels of training for department heads, physicians, physicians' assistants, nursing staff, and volunteers.
- Provide proprietary security upgrades for the system at a nominal fee.
- Improve video feeds for other systems in the hospital, such as video conferencing equipment, at the same time the new system is installed. This would show the superiority of the company's products and skills over those of the competition.

Step 4: Preparation Schedule

Once you have identified the main elements in your USP strategy, you can begin to fill in the proposal preparation schedule (see Exhibit 4.4). This schedule establishes specific dates for each task as well as for the first drafts of the technical, management, and time/cost sections of the proposal; the front matter; and the executive summary. Everyone on the proposal-writing team should know the deadlines for their sections of the proposal, the date the first draft of the complete document is to be assembled, and the date the document is to be turned over to management for review.

Step 5: Assignment of Tasks

Now that you have a concrete idea of your timelines, you can decide on the most effective and efficient assignment of tasks for members of the proposal team. If you are in charge of the proposal-writing process, part of your job is to know what tasks to delegate to which people. In some cases, for example, the person who originally had an idea is not the best person to develop it or write about it. Exhibit 4.5 shows a sample writing assignment schedule form.

In addition to making due dates very clear, it's a good idea to require routine progress reports from your proposal-writing staff. This approach has two major advantages. First, it allows you to detect quickly if someone is going off course. Even the best researchers and writers can occasionally get sidetracked. The sooner you catch their mistakes, the better your chances of keeping the proposal on course and on schedule.

The second benefit of routine progress reports is that they prevent people from procrastinating. If staff members must report regularly to you, they can't put off their tasks, or they'll have to

EXHIBIT 4.4

Proposal Preparation Schedule

RFP: Task	Week									
	1	2	3	4	5	6	7	8	9	10
Bid/no-bid decision										
Initial RFP analysis										
Proposal team selection										
Detailed RFP analysis										
Research; program development										
Development of time/cost table										
First draft of proposal selections										
Review and revision of proposal draft										
Front matter prepared										
Final text edited										
Text and graphics produced										
Proposal printed										
Proposal mailed (client presentation)										

explain why their work isn't done. If someone is not able to do an assigned task, you'll know about it early in the process, and you can quickly replace the person.

Before moving on to Chapter 5, review the Market and Competitive Analysis Form (Exhibit 4.6) on pp. 73–76. The form is designed to help you analyze your main competitors and compare your strengths and weaknesses against theirs.

Now you are ready to develop strategies for each of the sections in your program design. Chapter 5 presents a detailed outline for each section, what each section contains, and who in the client organization will read that section.

EXHIBIT 4.5
Form for Writing Assignments

Client: _____   Page ____ of ____

RFP page no.	Proposal page no.	Topic or section	Date due	Date received	First review	Final review	Writer	Comments

EXHIBIT 4.6
Market and Competitive Analysis Form

Instructions

1. Complete the information at the top of the form: competitor names, date, and the proposal manager responsible for the project.

2. In section A, answer the questions about you and your competitors in the context of your respective situations. Use a "+" sign to indicate an advantage that your firm possesses; a "o" to indicate that you and a competitor are equal in this area; and a "−" sign to indicate a disadvantage or gap your firm possesses compared to the competition.

3. In section B, answer the questions from the competitor's viewpoint, unless the question specifically asks you to compare the competitor's offering with your service.

4. In section C, fill in the summary of your findings.

Answer as many questions as you can. Whenever possible, research the questions you cannot answer using your current knowledge. The more high-quality answers you generate, the more information you will have that will enable you to prepare a winning proposal. And remember: What you don't know about your competitors can be as critical as what you do know. These voids in your knowledge point out where you are vulnerable to competition and reveal potential problems and opportunities for your firm.

Once the form is completed to the best of your ability, summarize your findings within the context of the entire form. This method allows you to conduct both a micro and macro analysis. Companies often make the mistake of looking at only one question at a time. You need to correlate the questions to obtain the best possible view of each competitor and your own firm.

Market and Competitive Analysis Form

Client: _____   Date: _____

Competitors' Names: _____   Proposal Manager:_____
_____

Section A	Our firm	Competitor 1	Competitor 2
1. Product differentiation from competitor's offerings			
2. Cyclicality of market segment (constant, seasonal, etc.)			

EXHIBIT 4.6 *(Continued)*

Section A	Our firm	Competitor 1	Competitor 2
3. Skills of the firms (all aspects)			
4. Product quality/service levels perceived by customers			
5. Flexibility of pricing structure			
6. Price competitiveness			
7. Barriers to entry			
8. Variety of applications and features			
9. Regulatory climate			
10. Risk in market segment			
11. Required investment to stay competitive			
12. Estimated profit margin ($)			
13. Estimated profit margin (%)			
14. Supplier power			

Section B

Competitor A: _____

1. Does this firm offer complementary services?

Their offering(s)   Your service equivalent

_____   _____

_____   _____

_____   _____

2. Do they have technological advantages over your products?

Their offering(s) and advantages   Your service equivalent

_____   _____

_____   _____

_____   _____

3. Do they add value to their services over yours?

Their offering and added value   Your service equivalent

_____   _____

_____   _____

_____   _____

EXHIBIT 4.6 *(Continued)*

4. What geographic area or niche are they targeting as their market?

List niches and service offering in each

Your service equivalent

_____   _____

_____   _____

_____   _____

5. Is their pricing strategy by individual service, total package, or both?

Describe their pricing strategy

_____

_____

6. What percent have they gone above or below the price of their service to make a sale?

Product offering and price variance

Your service equivalent

_____   _____

_____   _____

_____   _____

7. Do you feel this firm is cutting prices to increase bid acceptances for the long run or the short run?

Their service

Method of price cutting

_____   _____

_____   _____

_____   _____

8. What customer voids do their services fill that your service(s) do not?

Competitor's services (s)

Associated customer voids

_____   _____

_____   _____

_____   _____

9. What is their geographic coverage for their services (local, regional, national, international, etc.)?

_____

_____

10. Do customers perceive this firm's products as technologically superior or inferior to yours?

_____

_____

11. What service applications does this firm have above or below your offerings?

_____

_____

12. List specific target markets/segments/industries for each competitor service offered.

Service   Target market/segment/industry

_____   _____

_____   _____

_____   _____

13. What specific background advantages or disadvantages do their employees have compared to your firm's employees (e.g., degrees, experience, personal contacts)?

Their advantages   Their disadvantages

_____   _____

_____   _____

_____   _____

14. Compared to your firm, what technological advantages and disadvantages do they demonstrate?

_____

_____

_____

Section C

Summary

_____

_____

_____

_____

_____

_____

5

Developing Your Program Design

Step 6: Program Design—The Heart of Your Proposal
Your Compliance with the RFP
Three Parts of the Program Design
    Technical Section
        Who Reads the Technical Section?
        How Should This Section Look?
        Nondisclosure Statement
    Management Section
        Who Reads the Management Section?
        How Should This Section Look?
        Boilerplate Files
    Time/Cost Section
        Basic Budgets
        Cost Categories
        Direct Costs, Indirect Costs, General and Administrative Costs,
          and Profit/Fee
        Fixed, Variable, and Semivariable Costs
        Strategies for Estimating Costs
        Client Requests and Your Budget
        Presenting the Budget in the Proposal
        Separate Cost Volume
        Time Strategy
        Who Reads the Time/Cost Section?
        How Should This Section Look?
Appendixes in a Proposal
Summary of a Winning Program Design

Nicolle Herras met with the proposal team to go over the development of the program design.

"Everyone has done a great job developing a three-part approach to Everett's needs: first, we develop the interactive system to connect patients, health-care workers, and interpreters; second, we offer a partnership agreement with World Medical Interpreters; and third, we provide Everett's people with training and complete tech support. Our compliance review shows that we meet all of the requirements of the RFP.

"Now we need to nail down the program design and get the technical, management, and time/cost sections done. Everett has to know exactly what we're going to do, how we're going to do it, and how much time and money it will take to finish the job."

She consulted her laptop. "IT and Software are doing the technical section, and Finance will do the time/cost calculations. James and Laura, I'm giving you the management section. We have the information we need from the client about what they expect from us in terms of staff training, tech support, and backup."

Laura spoke up. "We turned up another issue in our talks with Everett. They need to make sure the interactive system that's built is in compliance with all government regulations and requirements. Do we have a compliance expert on staff?"

Ms. Herras nodded. "Bill Nalamwar from Legal. I'm adding him to the proposal team so he and his counterpart at Everett can coordinate with the federal regulator. His role will be part of our management strategy, so be sure you and James talk with Bill about the details."

James added, "Laura and I will take a look at past proposals and the swipe files to show Everett we have the necessary management expertise to organize and run a project like this. We'll need to know which of our consultants will be included in the proposal as project team members so we can call up their résumés."

Ms. Herras made a note. "I'll get back to you on that by Friday. I'm talking with Mr. Tagore this afternoon about who should be on the team. All right, what about time and cost calculations?"

One of the finance team members raised his hand. "From what Everett said in their RFP, they want a cost breakdown by major expense category. Also, they stipulated that general and administrative costs shouldn't be more than 15 percent of the total. We figure with a 10 percent cost overrun built in, we can achieve about a 12 to 15 percent profit margin on this project."

"Provided nothing goes seriously wrong," Ms. Herras said. She turned to the IT and software team. "Nothing is going to go seriously wrong, is it?"

Sy Warner shook his head amid the general laughter. "Not if we have anything to say about it. We can adapt the program that we used to build BioCom's interactive video system, which means we'll save a lot of time on the development end. We'll coordinate with Finance on the time and cost estimates. And I'll talk with Legal about putting the nondisclosure statement together."

Ms. Herras opened her project calendar. "All right, let's set due dates. I want drafts of the technical, management, and time/cost sections by Wednesday of next week. We've got one week before upper management reviews the drafts, so let's get it done!"

* * *

Step 6: Program Design—The Heart of Your Proposal

The service or product your firm offers the client represents your unique selling point (USP) in the proposal and must be expressed in the form of a program design. The design has several features:

- It identifies the real problem or need in the RFP and discusses it from the client's point of view. Whether this is simply the stated problem or a problem that your research reveals, you must cover all elements of the RFP.
- It tells the client *what* your company will do, by describing the approach you will take to address the problem(s).
- It tells the client *how* your company will do the job, by describing in more detail the services that your company will provide to meet the client's needs.
- It describes the staffing, time, and cost requirements needed to complete the job. The client will then have a good idea of *who* will do the work, *how long* it will take, and *how much* it will cost.

Your Compliance with the RFP

It's a good idea to do a final check of your overall compliance with the RFP requirements before you start putting together your complete program design. The client states these requirements in the "statement of work" or "scope of work" sections in the RFP. You want to avoid having a major requirement slip through the cracks in the flurry of gathering information, developing solutions and strategies, and creating your time/cost estimates. A checklist, such as the one shown in Exhibit 5.1, can help you identify any gaps in your program design. This should give you enough time to develop quality answers to fill in those gaps.

EXHIBIT 5.1
RFP Compliance Checklist

Requirement	Satisfies	Partially satisfies	Does not satisfy	Comments
1. Administrative requirements 　1.1 Improve care of non-English-speaking patients 　1.2 Use staff more efficiently 　1.3 Comply with government regulations	✓ (1.1) ✓ (1.2)	✓ (1.3)		1.3 Our compliance expert is working on details with Everett and government regulators
2. Technical requirements				
3. Equipment needs				
4. Training requirements				
5. Implementation requirements				
6. Budget requirements				
7. Other				

Three Parts of the Program Design

The technical section, management section, and staffing/time/cost section each contributes to the winning proposal. Pay careful attention to the details in each one. It won't matter if you have an outstanding technical strategy if your management strategy isn't adequate. This gap tells the client you may know *what* to do but not *how to get it done.* Many proposals are weak in this area. Keep in mind that you must sell the client on your *firm*, not just on your ideas.

Technical Section

The technical section has four goals:

- To show the client that your product or service can meet the RFP requirements.
- To demonstrate your understanding of the client's requirements and your firm's capacity to anticipate and resolve problems and to provide a workable solution.
- To assure the client that you can perform the work required.
- To describe the benefits the client will receive from the work.

The technical strategy in this section should convince the client that you have a superior grasp of the problems stated in the RFP and have devised a superior solution. The technical strategy may pick up other items from the general client needs/wants list prepared earlier. In this way, you begin to build a coordinated strategy that ties all three sections together and reinforces your overall differentiation strategy.

For example, the firm in the sample case may build into their software program a few features that will make it easier to market their solution to Everett administrators. These features could include the ability to access any test results while talking with interpreters or to patch in an off-site medical specialist to consult on a case. Such detailed strategies can work together to meet your client's needs/wants and to sell your proposal.

A critical success factor is keeping the detailed strategy for this section focused on the client's primary concern. In other words, what is the client's main goal?

- A more sophisticated technical solution?
- Greater safety in its operations?
- Increased productivity?
- Greater efficiency?
- Quicker delivery?
- More versatility?
- A combination of these elements?

Your background research should help you identify the client's primary concern. Make sure you can state the concern clearly in one or two sentences. For example, "The client wants an interactive video/voice call system to contact off-site interpreters quickly and easily, make more efficient use of staff time, promote better health care for non-English-speaking patients, and comply with government regulations. This strategy includes other features such as regular staff training, community outreach to non-English-speaking populations, and reduction in liability, hospital costs, and treatment errors."

Avoid the temptation to develop more than one technical strategy in a proposal. Generally, you need to focus on one main strategy rather than scatter your forces trying to develop two or more. However, you may have one or two minor strategies that are linked to the main strategy. For example, if improving customer service is the main strategy, a minor strategy might be developing special promotions and customer giveaways.

Who Reads the Technical Section?

In general, the people who developed the RFP and who are in charge of the project will read and evaluate the technical section. Their primary focus will be on the technical details of your proposed solution; they may not have a marketing or sales perspective. However, they should be able to understand the marketing and sales benefits of your technical product or service as well as pricing models and market strategies.

Keep in mind that although your readers will be competent in their individual fields, they may not be experts in your technology. When writing the technical section, don't assume a level of knowledge about your work that the readers may not have. Be careful to explain terms, concepts, processes, and any software/hardware that is unique to your company, field, or industry. You do not need to talk down to your audience, but take into consideration the readers' point of view when you write the proposal.

Your background research should tell you the level of knowledge and expertise of those who will be evaluating the technical section. Do not make any assumptions without doing research.

How Should This Section Look?

Although the format will vary somewhat depending on the RFP requirement, a technical section generally contains the following:

- *Section overview:* Introduces the content of the technical section and acts as a road map to help readers find specific topics in the text.
- *Introduction:* Presents your understanding and interpretation of the client's problem.
- *Solution:* Explains your approach to the problem, why you developed the solution that you did, the main features of the solution, and the benefits to the client.
- *Product or service description:* Provides additional details of the product or service your solution offers to the client.
- *Installation and implementation plan:* Outlines how you will install any necessary equipment or processes and how you will measure whether they are implemented and used successfully.
- *Project organization and key project staff information:* Describes how the project will be organized and introduces the key personnel from your firm who will work with the client.

In addition to the information above, many technical sections also include a discussion of assumptions made during the proposal-writing process. In some cases, an RFP may not be specific enough, the client may not know the answers to your questions, or your background research does not provide the missing data. As a result, you may need to make certain assumptions to fill in the gaps. It is common practice to keep working on your proposal even when you do not have all the information you need.

Assumptions should be based on your firm's expertise in the client's problem area. You will need to provide support or documentation for these assumptions in your proposal so the client understands your thinking.

Also, avoid the trap of "assuming away" problems. If you learn that a client manager has objections to your program design, for example, don't assume that you will be able to answer whatever questions he or she may raise. You could find out the hard way—in the client presentation—that you don't have the answers. Prepare yourself and your team to overcome objections with reasonable and well-supported responses.

Nondisclosure Statement.
At times, you may need to go into some detail in the technical section. To prevent the client, or a competitor, from using your proprietary information, you can include a nondisclosure statement with the proposal (see Exhibit 5.2). Consult your legal department or a lawyer about the proper wording of the statement.

EXHIBIT 5.2
Nondisclosure Statement

1. *Statement placed on company documents and other materials:*
   PRIVATE

   The information contained herein should not be disclosed to unauthorized persons. It is meant solely for the use of authorized Everett Hospital employees.

2. *Statement included in company proposal:*

   Attached is the November 20— Everett Hospital plan. This document is the responsibility of C. B. Berkowitz and is not to be reproduced in any form. It contains certain private and confidential data concerning the Everett Hospital plan.

3. *Separate statement to be signed by the client company:*
   NONDISCLOSURE STATEMENT

   Everett Hospital agrees to keep all information contained in this proposal confidential. It is understood that the proposal contains proprietary information developed by Integrated Medical Systems, Inc., specifically for Everett Hospital and that this material is not to be reproduced or disclosed to any unauthorized personnel.

A nondisclosure statement can appear in several forms. It may be a statement included on the title page and every page thereafter of the proposal. It also can be placed on all preparation materials you develop within your firm. At times, a nondisclosure statement is simply a signed agreement between your company and the client that forbids the client from disclosing or revealing to anyone outside the project the information contained in your proposal or learned through discussions with you.

If you have any doubt about how clients will handle material you include in your technical section, have them sign a nondisclosure statement. If they refuse to do so, you must then assess the risk/benefit of submitting the proposal and possibly losing proprietary information.

Management Section

In the management section, you explain how you expect to work with the client to achieve the client's goals. Your management plan is based on your experience and the client's RFP. How detailed you make the plan depends on the level of detail the client asks for in the RFP. Even if you provide only upper management level details in the proposal, this information will serve as the basis for your full management plan after you have won the contract.

The management strategy should leave no doubts in the client's mind that your company will be able to manage and implement the solution. The management section has two goals:

- To show the client that your firm has the experience, personnel, and resources needed to do the work you describe in your proposal.
- To demonstrate your firm's understanding of the details of the project, such as coordinating work between your staff and the client's staff, installing equipment or processes, training client personnel, devising test procedures, providing technical support, and monitoring results.

You may not always have a separate management section. Depending on the RFP, you may include your management strategy or information about your firm in the technical section. Some RFPs, for example, request information about a firm's management, resources, and experience but not about managerial function such as installation, testing, monitoring, and so forth. For the purposes of this chapter, however, we are assuming that you need to write a separate management section in response to an RFP.

All too often, the management plan is one of the most neglected areas in proposal planning. Why? The answer is surprisingly simple: the proposal team is focused on developing a product or service and on the nuts and bolts of who will do the job, how long it will take, and how much it will cost. As a result, the management strategy has no staff champion. More often than not, at the last moment, someone hastily writes a few pages, slaps them into the proposal, and—voilá!—a "management plan."

The management strategy is important for two reasons: (1) it can be another way to sell your firm and differentiate yourself from the competition, and (2) it shows the client *how* you intend to get the job done. Your management strategy must support the technical strategy and complement your proposal's differentiation strategy. You can use this section to stress your competence and USP in various ways. Some typical management strategies include:

- Emphasizing your firm's superior management experience in producing similar products or services in the past.
- Assuring the client that top management will have direct control of the project.
- Demonstrating that you have exceptionally qualified personnel who will work on the client's project.
- Convincing the client that you can provide superior quality control during each phase of the project.
- Emphasizing your manager's expertise in implementation and follow-through. The work doesn't end with the development of a product or service; you will ensure that the client is satisfied with how it performs in operation.

Developing this section forces you to think through the "best case/worst case" scenarios in terms of possible delays, setbacks, conflicts, and misunderstandings. It gives you a chance to ask "what if?" questions and create contingency plans should your original management plan run into problems. For instance, what if a supplier can't meet a delivery date, or a software program requires more than the usual debugging, or you lose a key staff member in the midst of the project? Devising contingency plans for these situations can save you a great deal of time, embarrassment, and financial loss. Generally, contingency plans are not written into the proposal but are kept in a separate file. All the client needs to know is that you have thought through a solid management plan.

In some cases, the management strategy can be the section where you stand out from the competition. Remember, the fundamental goal of a proposal is to sell your firm to the client. In some instances, your technical and time/cost sections may be similar to other proposals that the client receives. In such cases, a well-thought-out management strategy could make the difference between success or failure.

Who Reads the Management Section?

Generally, the same people who read the technical section will evaluate the management section. Once you have convinced the client about *what* you can do, you must convince them that you know *how* to do it. As a result, the technical and management sections must be written so that they are consistent and support one another.

For example, your technical section may emphasize how easily a new billing program can be integrated into the client's computer system. But your management section contains a highly complex plan to oversee implementation and monitoring of the program. The client will naturally want to know this: if you say the process is so easy, why does the program take so much time and effort to install and run? The client may think twice about awarding you the job.

Make sure your proposal sections are internally consistent. If you claim in the technical section that your solution is an easy one, your management section must provide a clear, simple plan to implement it.

How Should This Section Look?

There are several ways to organize a management section. At the least it should provide an introduction to the management plan; an outline of your firm's capabilities; which personnel from your firm will be responsible for overseeing the project and for implementation, training, and monitoring; and what the client's responsibilities are. A suggested outline might contain the following:

1. *Introduction:* An overview of the entire section that gives the client a snapshot of what the section contains.
2. *Project management approach:* A description of the approach that you feel will best direct the project successfully, whether team or project management, co-management with client personnel, or some other approach. Remember, the final management plan is often worked out between the submitting firm and the client. Your initial plan submitted with the proposal is your best evaluation regarding how the project should be managed.
3. *Project organization and responsibilities:* How the project stages and tasks will be organized and who will be responsible for accomplishing each stage or task. This is the heart of any management strategy and should be thoroughly reviewed for completeness and credibility.

    If the project requires replacing a client's existing technology, product, or system, you will need to outline how and when the old system will be converted to the new one. Make sure you provide examples of how you have handled similar projects in the past.
4. *Management of subcontractors:* In some cases, part of the project may need to be completed by subcontractors. These vendors will require close supervision. You may or may not want to mention the need for subcontractors in the proposal. This is a decision that will have to be made on a case-by-case basis. Some clients may consider the use of subcontractors to be an indication that your firm is incapable of doing the job. Others may see it as a sign of resourcefulness. Your knowledge of the client will guide you in this matter.
5. *Project schedules:* A critical management task is to keep the project on track and on budget. The schedules must reflect realistic estimates based on your knowledge of your firm, experience with similar projects, and client resources. Typically, you would list tasks, and even subtasks in some cases, with estimated start and stop dates, estimated hours/days required to complete each task, and the personnel assigned

to each task. Project schedules are usually refined after a contract is awarded. Your task for the proposal is to make the schedules as realistic as possible based on the information you have at hand and on your experience.

6. *Implementation, training, testing, and monitoring:* This stage is critical to the ongoing success of the project. The client must be satisfied with the initial solution as well as its long-term performance. If required, the management plan must include details for training personnel and for testing and monitoring the product or service over a set period, usually three to six months. However, in some cases the time frame may be up to a year or more.

7. *Project staffing:* Your management plan should provide not only your best estimate of how many staff members will be required for the project but also whether the staff includes outside contractors and/or client personnel. Some of the questions you should address include: What qualifications do the project staff need to have? Will they require any training before the project starts or at any stage along the way? How will your staff and outside or client staff work together? You must clearly spell out the roles and responsibilities of all staff members, whether they are from your firm, from subcontractors, or from the client organization.

8. *Documentation for products:* Include any manuals or other instructional materials that go with the products in your proposal. You can describe the documentation in your management section and supply manuals on CD, DVD, or through downloadable files on your Web site. User documentation is an important part of a winning proposal.

9. *Payment terms and warranties:* If the RFP requests that you include payment terms in the management section, outline clearly the payment schedule for the project. In some cases, the schedule will be discussed beforehand with the client. Some common payment terms include a percent of the fee, such as 25 percent, on signing the contract and regular payments at agreed-upon benchmarks. These might include product delivery and installation, successful testing and operation, completion of in-house training, and the client's formal acceptance of the product.

If you are offering a warranty for your work, you will need to describe when the warranty starts, how long it will last, and what it will cover. The terms you set and the terms a client expects may not always be the same. As a result, the final details of a warranty are usually negotiated between the submitting firm and the client.

10. *References from other clients and a history or other pertinent information about your firm:* References and key information about your firm help strengthen your firm's credibility with the client. If a client learns, for example, that the leading firms in their industry recommend your work, that fact could tip the balance in your favor.

Likewise, your firm may have developed a widely used process or product or acquired a high level of expertise in the client's field. Highlight this information in the management strategy section to emphasize your credibility as uniquely qualified to solve the client's problems and create realistic benefits.

You can also invite the client to ask questions or comment on the management plan in your proposal. Keep in mind that the management strategy section lets the client evaluate *how* you will do the work. Make sure that question is answered to the client's fullest satisfaction.

Boilerplate Files.
Several items in the management section can be prepared from boilerplate files. These files include résumés, company descriptions, client references, and other material that will be used over and over in your proposals (see sample boilerplate résumés in Appendix C). The files can be easily adapted to the requirements of each RFP. For example, suppose a client wants to tie in their online marketing service with several social media platforms. You would stress your staff members' Web site and social networking expertise, their software applications skills, their knowledge of online marketing practices, and their prior work on related projects.

Boilerplate files can help to streamline the proposal-writing process. Some of these files include:

• *Project management strategy:* Over time, you may discover that a particular management strategy works well for your firm.

This file could contain a general description of that strategy, including a statement of what work you will perform, a management plan, and work schedules.

- *Organization charts, flow charts, other exhibit materials:* You may use organization or flow charts to show your firm's structure and method of operation, how your project management system works, or any other topic you routinely illustrate in an RFP. You can change, adapt, or re-create these illustrations for specific RFPs. (See Chapter 7: Producing Your Proposal.)
- *Staff résumés:* You may want to have several versions of all staff members' résumés available so that you can stress different skills and experience they have in different areas. Résumé files should be kept on senior management staff, project managers, technical personnel, product developers, and any relevant outside staff you regularly use.
- *Contracts and nondisclosure/confidentiality statements:* This file would include standard forms for agreements you make with subcontractors, service companies, outside consultants, suppliers, team agreements, and the like.
- *Training programs:* If your products or services require training client personnel, a boilerplate description of your training program could save time when you write the proposal. This file would include an explanation of your training approach, setup of classes, presentation of material, and expected results.
- *Client references:* RFPs usually require three or more client references attesting to the quality of your firm's work and overall performance. The information provided in these references generally includes a brief history of the client firm; the reason your company was chosen for the job; what product or service you provided that is still in place; and the title, name, phone number, and/or address of a direct contact in the client firm.

Time/Cost Section

Especially in today's business environment, time/cost strategies must be factored into the proposal process from the beginning. Gone are the days when clients had surplus cash to throw at a problem in order to find the best solution. You can be sure that the client's financial officer will be scrutinizing every proposal for unrealistic estimates, hidden costs, and padded figures. With current operating and profit margins so thin, clients may put cost above other considerations when deciding between two similar proposals. In such cases, focusing on value-added services may be the best approach when writing the proposal. Clients may select a less sophisticated product or service simply because they can afford it. Or they may ask for the bidders to resubmit their bids based on a lower cost strategy.

Bidding on state or federal contracts (e.g., for the Department of Defense) is a world all its own. Pricing is often based on the General Services Administration price list. Because government bids are complex to prepare, companies generally have a specialist on staff or hire consultants to put together the time/cost section for government proposals.

Your time/cost strategy must accomplish three critical objectives:

1. *Demonstrate that you have an understanding of the client's financial situation.* Does the client have a fixed budget? A company estimate? Other resources from which to draw if needed? Your strategy should reflect your background research of the client's resources and show an appreciation for the client's circumstances.
2. *Cover the actual costs of the project.* This includes creating a final product or service, plus other services your firm may provide, such as implementation and monitoring. These cost estimates can be based on historical data of similar past projects (adjusted for inflation), additional outside staff that may be needed, equipment required, and so forth.
3. *Earn a profit for your firm.* Although this may seem too obvious to mention, it is surprising how many companies either break even or actually lose money on the projects they win. Remember, each proposal must support your company's mission and long-term business strategy. To do so, you must have a realistic idea of what you need to charge to earn a profit on every job and what your profit margin needs to be. The profit margin may change from one job to the next.

These three objectives will help you avoid the temptation to cut costs or corners simply to submit a low bid. The right strategy can help you win the more lucrative contracts.

Those who believe that the best cost strategy is "lower, lower, lower" may win their share of contracts, but lose out on the higher-paying projects. There are three reasons why this is the case.

First, the client may need to spend their allocated funds before a stated deadline—for instance, the end of the fiscal year. Although less common than in the past, this situation means that the client is mostly concerned about spending all their funds for fear that future allocations will be set at a lower level. As long as your proposal costs appear reasonable to the client, money will not be the deciding factor.

Second, the lowest bid might not win the contract when the client has a fixed budget for the project. In this case, the client's main concern will be getting the most value for their money. The client will be looking primarily for high-quality solutions at a cost within an established budget.

Third, if your cost estimate is too far below your competitors' estimates, the client may feel that you cannot deliver a quality product or that you do not really understand the problem in the RFP. Either way, your proposal loses.

Having said this, however, we do not mean to suggest that you shouldn't try to find ways to lower costs where feasible. How and when you decide to do so depends on each individual project. For example, if you lower your fixed costs for an RFP, the freed-up funds can be used to add features to your product or service, which may make your proposal more attractive to the client.

You can lower your costs in several ways. One of the most effective is by designing an innovative system, product, or service that produces actual cost savings that can be passed on to the client. If this approach is not possible, you can attempt to minimize overhead costs as you work, which will result in a lower overhead rate and lower total costs to the client. If the RFP requires a labor-intensive product or service as a solution, the company with the lowest overhead rate usually wins the contract. Finally, consider other ways to reduce costs, such as subcontracting, forming joint teaming agreements, and other creative methods of getting the job done while maintaining quality and satisfying the client.

Basic Budgets.

When developing a budget, you have some choice in how you set up your cost categories and expense items. Budgets can be itemized or nonitemized as well as fixed or flexible:

1. *Itemized budgets:* These budgets provide a detailed breakdown of the project expenses. They tell the client more specifically how much each part of the project is going to cost. As you are developing your proposal, it's a good idea to develop an itemized budget for yourself. You can see where the money is going and make adjustments to control expenses. The itemized budget gives you detailed information to answer a client's questions about how parts of the proposal budget were developed.

2. *Nonitemized budgets:* These budgets are less detailed and usually much shorter. You provide the client with the expenses to show how you derived the figures in your proposal. A nonitemized budget consolidates costs into bigger categories. You can use your itemized budget as the basis for putting together a nonitemized budget. Proposals often include nonitemized budgets for one simple reason: many firms consider their methods of calculating costs as proprietary information. Exhibit 5.3 provides an example of itemized and nonitemized budgets.

3. *Fixed budgets:* When you prepare a fixed budget, you are basically telling the client that you will provide a product or service for a fixed cost. That cost will not change, even if production, installation, training, or any other costs increase. You cannot go back to the client and ask them to renegotiate the fee or cover your additional expenses.

4. *Flexible budgets:* These budgets can be adjusted to reflect changes in project costs. The adjustments can be made on a monthly, quarterly, or yearly basis, depending on what you and the client have agreed upon. At the end of each period, projected costs are compared to actual costs, and the budget is adjusted for the next period. Usually the client negotiates an upper and lower limit to these cost variances. These budgets are commonly used for ongoing or multipart projects where it is difficult to predict what the actual costs are going to be over the life of the project.

EXHIBIT 5.3

Itemized Budget and Nonitemized Budget

Itemized Budget

Project: Everett Hospital

Date: 10/12/20—

Personnel		
Salaries	$218,000	
Fringe (27.8%)	60,604	
Subcontractor	14,000	
Subtotal		$292,604
Hardware Equipment		
Interactive voice/video	$24,000	
Hardware rental other	12,000	
Communication/telephone/DSL/T1	5,432	
Subtotal		41,432
Prototype Field Testing		8,677
Project Management		
Travel	$15,775	
Training — executive	4,125	
Training — user	11,110	
Documentation — summary form	1,450	
Documentation — detailed form	4,400	
Follow-up details	25,000	
Subtotal		61,860
General and Administrative (G&A)		
Supplies	$6,000	
Office expenses	13,500	
Depreciation, taxes, insurance	5,087	
Subtotal		24,587
% Overhead to Apply ($)		20,439
Total Direct Cost		$449,599
Total Indirect Cost (17.2%)		77,331
TOTAL COSTS		$526,930

Nonitemized Budget

Project: Everett Hospital

Date: 10/12/20—

Personnel — Salaries	$292,604	
Hardware Equipment	41,432	
Prototype Field Testing	8,677	
Project Management	61,860	
G&A[*]	24,587	
% Overhead to Apply ($)	20,439	
Total Direct Cost		$449,599
Total Indirect Cost	77,331	
TOTAL COSTS		$526,930

[*]Note: Salaries are not included in this category but are shown in a separate line.

Cost Categories.

There are several broad cost categories that you need to address when developing cost estimates for your proposal. Cost categories can be set up in terms of direct costs, indirect costs, general and administrative costs, and profit/fee. You can also set up the categories in terms of fixed, variable, and semivariable costs. The approach you choose may depend on several factors such as RFP requirements, the nature of your company's business, and your finance officer's preferences.

Direct Costs, Indirect Costs, General and Administrative Costs, and Profit/Fee.

- *Direct costs* are those that can be charged to a specific contract. Examples of direct costs include employee compensation, materials and supplies, travel, telephone expenses, and printing.
- *Indirect costs* are those costs associated with running your business that cannot be charged to a particular project. These expenses, such as utilities, rent, benefits, and salaries, must be absorbed by all the projects that your company takes on throughout the year.
- *General and administrative (G&A)* costs include marketing, legal fees, research and development, and general corporate expenses.
- *Profit/fee costs* are as follows: the *fee* is the cost to your firm of completing the project plus a certain percentage over costs. The *profit* is the fee less all costs associated with the project. You must be able to forecast your firm's expenses in the three areas above to calculate your profit/fee percentage as a profit rate on material and a fixed dollar rate for profit on labor.

Note that your profit margin should be built into your costs. It should *not* be determined ahead of time, and then allocated equally to each section of the project. You can easily price yourself out of a contract using this method. For example, some RFPs will state explicitly that general and administrative expenses cannot exceed 15 percent of the total cost of the bid. Some projects will require higher profit margins than others because they may be more labor-intensive or more difficult to perform.

Fixed, Variable, and Semivariable Costs.
The advantage of identifying which costs are fixed, variable, and semivariable is that you can anticipate which costs are likely to change over the life of the project. This information will help you estimate expenses for the proposal budget and make it easier for you to calculate your profit margin. This method of categorizing expenses is especially appropriate for clients that have production facilities.

*   *Fixed costs* are expenses that will remain stable over the life of the project. These include rent, equipment costs, depreciation, and management and staff salaries. You have little ability to affect these costs.
*   *Variable costs* are expenses that fluctuate during the project. These costs include travel, communications, supplies and materials, development of products and services, installation and training, and the like.
*   *Semivariable costs* are those that are associated with fixed or variable costs. For example, the cost of video equipment may increase by only 5 percent, but the cost of replacing individual video parts may increase by 15 percent.

Strategies for Estimating Costs.
As a general rule, you should assign all project costs to a category as you develop your in-house budget to track expenses. This way you are more likely to estimate your costs accurately and to end up with a realistic budget for your proposal.

Although there are several techniques for estimating costs, two of the more commonly used methods are the bottom-up approach and the top-down approach. The bottom-up approach is widely used for projects in which costs are not the main concern. In this technique, the cost of each of the steps in the program design is determined and added to obtain a total cost.

The top-down technique is used more often when the project is cost-sensitive, if you have a good idea of the client's budget for the project, or if you know what your competitors are likely to bid. Using the top-down approach, you target a final cost estimate before beginning the project design. A percentage of this target cost is assigned to each task for the final project.

Whether you use the bottom-up or top-down approach, carefully review the dollar amounts and/or percentages in your estimate to be sure that you cover all costs and that they are reasonable for the RFP.

Some firms find it useful to develop a pro-forma income statement that details all costs of a project. This method, though more time-consuming than the other approaches, will provide you with more accurate cost estimates. If you are able to determine what the client is willing to expend on the project, your estimated dollar profit and return on investment can easily be calculated. This method also helps you determine whether your final profit or loss from the project is worth your time and effort.

As an alternative to preparing a pro-forma income statement, you could prepare your cost statement or cost budget by major expense categories. These are the figures you would generally include in your proposal; detailed pro-forma income statements are usually used for in-house analysis only.

Even though the cost statement or budget is listed by major expense categories, it is strongly recommended that you perform a detailed cost analysis so that you do not miss any cost categories. A shortened list of cost categories, also known as a line-item budget, is shown in Exhibit 5.4. A line-item budget is simply a list of all expense categories that apply to the project.

Once you have completed your budget for the proposal, use variance analysis to keep track of cost overruns or underruns. This approach allows you or your firm's management to take corrective action immediately on any problems that arise to prevent them from becoming major crises.

Client Requests and Your Budget.

It should be noted that the client can request a detailed breakdown of any category listed in a cost estimate or ask you to justify your costs. The client may want to see how you arrived at a figure. For example, you may list rental expenses for a four-week project at $6,400. The client wants the total broken down by rental item:

Rental Expense:

Video cameras	–	$1,200 per week	=	$4,800
Studio lights	–	$100 per week	=	$400
Audio package	–	$300 per week	=	$1,200

EXHIBIT 5.4

Shortened List of Cost Categories

Project: Everett Hospital

Date: 10/12/20—

Proposal Team Compensation—Salaries	$218,000
Interactive Voice/Video Hardware	24,000
Subcontract Services	14,000
Hardware Rental—Other	12,000
Supplies	6,000
Depreciation Taxes, Insurance	5,087
Training and Education	15,235
Prototype Field Testing	8,677
Office Expenses	13,500
Telephone/Capital DSL/T1	5,432
Travel	15,775
% of Overhead to Apply ($)	20,439
Follow-up Expenses	25,000
Fringe Benefits (27.8%)	60,604
Documentation	5,850
Total Indirect Costs (17.2%)	77,331
TOTAL COSTS	$526,930

In some cases, you may have hard and soft costs in your budget. Hard costs are those that can be easily quantified and therefore are less likely to be challenged by the client. For instance, if Integrated Medical Systems can improve call routing efficiency, they can cite a reduction in system costs of $300 per month. Soft costs are those that are more difficult to quantify. For example, improved call routing efficiency might also help staff morale, but by how much? What are the direct benefits of improved morale to Everett's bottom line?

Be aware that if your budget contains several soft cost items, the client is likely to challenge them. The best way to support soft costs is to cite third-party sources—testimonials from previous clients, historical industry data, government or academic statistics, or experts in the field. For example, Integrated Medical Systems could back up their claim by saying, "Three hospitals in California that used this system reported a significant increase in morale, which resulted in a 10 percent increase in productivity." The best approach is to assume that your soft cost items will be challenged—so be prepared to back up your claims.

If you have trouble developing a cost estimate for a particular project or cannot find sufficient information on the client's proposed budget, you may want to consider developing your response to the RFP in stages instead of submitting a single response to the bid. For instance, in the first stage you would bid for doing the job well but with no extras or add-ons. This would cover only the baseline product or service needed to meet the RFP requirements. The second stage would involve a bid that included the most appropriate and attractive add-ons you believe the client would want. The final stage would be a bid for a "top-of-the-line" job with all the features and add-ons for maximum value (similar to a rate sheet).

Each of these stages is priced out separately but developed in a modular format. Each stage can be performed quickly and easily without rebuilding the prior stages. This strategy presents the client with more possibilities than a single response would and offers them a wider range of choices. The client can take advantage of this type of schedule and can contract for the job in phases as funds become available.

If your cost estimates come in consistently high and are too far above the acceptable range for the bid, you will need to find ways of reducing your costs. These include staging your proposal as described above, using innovative systems or approaches that lower your costs, finding ways to lower your overhead expenses, and, if all else fails, discounting. You can use new-account discounts, straight discounts, large-quantity discounts, and the like. However, one of the major drawbacks to this method is that clients may come to expect discounts in the future as well. You will have to obtain your profit from other jobs, which may force you to price other RFPs higher than you ordinarily would.

If you cannot trim your costs to fit the contract range, consider walking away from the job. If winning a bid is going to have a negative impact on your firm, you may be better off turning the project down. Remember, your primary objective is to support your company's mission and long-term marketing strategy.

Presenting the Budget in the Proposal.

The budget is a critical part of your sales and marketing message to the client. Take time to decide how you will present the budget in the proposal and what you want the client to take away from your discussion of costs.

Where you place the budget in your proposal depends on several factors. If the budget is a brief, nonitemized list of costs, you can place it in the body of the proposal, usually in the management section. You can include a short summary of how you arrived at the budget. This gives the client a good overview of expenses and the basis for their calculation. Such an approach works well for many smaller jobs or short-term contracts.

If you provide a highly detailed itemized budget, you are better off placing it in an appendix. You can then provide a brief summary of cost categories in the body of the proposal, with a reference to the appendix. This approach is more appropriate to larger, multipart contracts or contracts that will take more than a year to complete. The client will need to factor in the long-term cost of the work to calculate their return on investment.

No matter where you place the budget, you should present it as a stand-alone document with three parts:

1. The opening paragraphs present the budget and discuss the costs of the project. You might have a point that you wish your budget to prove, such as you are able to offer significant cost savings to the client because of the way you have structured your cost items. Or you may want to justify certain costs by explaining what value or benefits the client will receive for the money. Again, this is your opportunity to sell your firm.
2. The body of the budget shows cost categories and supports any claims you make about expenses or benefits to the client. You can add explanatory remarks or notes to any budget item. Generally, the client will not be as familiar with the cost categories as you are, so it's a good idea to anticipate questions the client might raise and answer them in the proposal. This also gives you an opportunity to explain how certain costs were calculated.
3. The closing, which may be only a few sentences, reinforces your main points and emphasizes the soundness of your budget. Avoid sounding apologetic or wavering in your conclusions. The client will be quick to pick up on this and realize that they can attack the budget and probably get you to lower your

estimates. You want to come to the client from a position of strength: "This is what it's going to cost to do the work."

Never forget that budgets are one of the most critical parts of any proposal. Particularly in today's business environment, clients will be scrutinizing your cost items carefully, looking for ways to cut expenses and get more for less money. Be prepared to support your budget items with sound reasons and examples that will also convince the client that you have considered their financial situation as well. But remember, the more money a client cuts from your budget, the harder it will be for you to complete the project.

Separate Cost Volume.

In some instances, you may wish to create a separate volume containing cost estimates and pricing. This may be particularly wise when you want the client to evaluate the technical and management sections without being influenced by the cost. Generally, you make only one copy of this separate volume, marked *confidential* and *proprietary*, and give it to top management or to the senior accounting or finance officer.

In rare instances, the cost volume may be submitted after the technical and management sections of the proposals have been evaluated. This may be true when cost estimates for a large proposal cannot be completed by the RFP due date. For example, equipment prices and other cost data may not be available in time or may change rapidly. If you need more time to develop the cost section, discuss this with the client. It is always best to keep the client informed about your progress. No one likes unpleasant surprises.

Time Strategy.

Time strategies are based on your firm's prior experience with similar work and/or on careful research of similar types of projects. In some cases, such as software development, precise time estimates may be difficult to make. However, you should be able to establish some type of realistic schedule for the project. You may want to cite similar projects in a footnote or list them in a table to justify to the client why you have confidence in your time estimates.

A more sophisticated method for time estimation and reduction used by many firms is a technique called PERT/CPM (Program

Evaluation and Review Technique with the Critical Path Method). This method identifies key tasks and subordinate tasks and organizes a time schedule so that key tasks are accomplished first. A discussion of PERT/CPM is beyond the scope of this book, but there are many operations research books that describe this method in detail.

The format for project schedules can vary from simple timeline graphs to more elaborate graphics. We recommend you keep the format clear and simple. For example:

Schedule for Software Development: October 14—December 17

Design and program development	October 14—November 3
Program testing and debugging	November 4— November 24
Field testing/refinement	November 25—December 17

The more technically difficult or abstract the project (e.g., improve worker efficiency and motivation), the longer the solution may take. Solutions to more concrete projects, such as redesigning work flow or developing a new distribution network, generally take less time to develop.

Who Reads the Time/Cost Section?

In general, the accounting or finance group evaluates the time/cost section, although eventually everyone on the RFP committee or group will look it over. Time and cost evaluation in large companies is usually a formal process overseen by members of senior management. This group will compare your cost estimates and time schedules with those of your competitors and against the client's own experience with similar projects.

Your background research should determine whether the client has a formal or informal time/cost evaluation process, and the level of sophistication of the people who will be doing the review. This information can help you decide how much information to include and how you should organize and present the time and cost data.

For example, when the client has a more formal time/cost evaluation process, you would break down the schedule and cost estimates into more detail, providing justification for each item. For a more informal process, you might emphasize broader time and cost categories, focusing on key schedule dates and the costs associated with each date. In this case, the client is not as interested in how you arrived at the figures as they are in what the figures cover and when payments to your firm will be due.

How Should This Section Look?

The time/cost section may be as simple as a list of equipment or services with the prices included and a brief work schedule. On the other hand, it may include a detailed budget with your cost-estimating techniques and a breakdown of tasks and subtasks.

Your time/cost section usually contains the following information:

- *Schedule of the work, generally with key completion dates for each stage:* This tells the client what will be done and when. Breaking the project down into stages gives the client a better idea of the time, staff, and resources required to complete each stage successfully.
- *Cost summary:* This can be a nonitemized budget that summarizes all costs for such categories as equipment; licensing fees; hardware and software; maintenance; project management; training; and implementation, administration, testing, and monitoring. In addition it lists any discounts available. You can present a more detailed itemized budget in an appendix to the proposal.
- *Cost totals:* This presents an overview of the bottom-line total costs of the project.
- *Delivery and payment schedules:* This lists the products or services that will be delivered to the client and a payment schedule for work done and/or products or services delivered.
- *Standard terms and conditions:* These let the client know under what conditions payment should be made and what is expected of both parties should there be delays or problems with the project. This part is, in effect, a contract for services between you and the client. Your firm may have a boilerplate agreement that can be inserted in each proposal. The terms can be modified during negotiations.

The time/cost section of the proposal can be the most difficult section to develop. Not only are issues of scheduling and pricing hotly debated among the proposal team members, but also the section is generally developed when the team is near exhaustion. As a result, this section often requires more time and effort than expected at the outset of the proposal-writing process.

Make sure that you are well prepared by gathering pricing information early in the process and by making changes as the proposal is developed. Also, keep management interference to a minimum, if possible. Pricing is one area that will unfailingly attract the attention of upper management. They may want to review the figures or help to develop the section without having sufficient information about the scope and program design of the proposal. Being concerned with the bottom line, they may criticize the cost estimates or suggest cuts or additions that are not in line with the rest of the proposal.

Last, the client may request changes that will affect your time/cost estimates. For example, the client may want to add or subtract tasks to the original RFP that will reduce or extend the timeline for the project. These changes may also force you to subtract or add staff to the project.

In another instance, a client may want to add or subtract equipment, services, or processes; reduce or increase the scope of the project; or make unexpected requests that will force you to restructure the entire time/cost section. Keep in mind that if the job is one you definitely want, you may be able to outlast your competition by responding to each request with timely, professional answers.

Appendixes in a Proposal

Appendixes contain supplemental material that can be used to support or illustrate your technical, management, or time/cost sections or simply provide additional information to the client. Appendixes are named by letter, not numbers: Appendix A, Appendix B, and so on.

Material included in the appendixes is generally too detailed to put into the main body of the proposal. A complete list of equipment and parts pricing, for example, is suitable for an appendix but may be too long and detailed for the cost section of the proposal. In the text, you point out where this additional material can be found: "For a complete list of equipment prices, see Appendix A." Each appendix is referenced in the appropriate section of the proposal. If you add or subtract appendixes, be sure that references to these appendixes in the proposal text are also added or deleted. It can be embarrassing for a client to ask "Where is Appendix C?" when you eliminated it from the proposal.

The appendixes should contain only material that is directly related to the proposal. Resist the temptation to include information that is nice to know but not essential for the client to have. For example, the client needs to know why you have chosen to use a more expensive video camera, but the client doesn't need to know the history of the manufacturer. Also, make sure that you have put all the important data in the text. Do not depend on appendix material to fulfill an RFP requirement.

Some information generally included in appendixes includes:

- Industry surveys, reports, and statistics
- Company brochures and other data
- Sample contracts and letters of agreement
- Sample training class content and schedules
- Policies and guidelines
- Reprints of relevant articles or technical data sheets
- Annual reports and financial data

Summary of a Winning Program Design

Never forget that the program design is the heart of your proposal. Your winning program design must do *all* of the following:

- Convince clients that you understand their problems even better than they do and that you have a USP to solve those problems.
- Present a concise, detailed plan for solving those problems within the requirements of the RFP. The plan and all detailed strategies should emphasize your strengths to the client.
- Provide technical, management, and time/cost strategies that tell the client what will be done, how it will be done, who will do it, how long it will take, and how much it will cost.
- Convince the client beyond any doubt that you will be able to implement the program design. If you or your client has any serious reservations about this, you should think twice about submitting your proposal.

- Above all, your program design should sell the client on your *firm*—not just on your product and service ideas. The program should state clearly what benefits the client will receive from your proposed solutions.

6

Writing the Front Matter and Executive Summary

The deadline for submitting the formal proposal to Everett Hospital was fast approaching, and the team was working hard on the final details. Top management had approved the program design, and Mr. Tagore had given Ms. Herras a list of key points to include in the executive summary.

"You've all done exceptional work so far," Ms. Herras told the proposal team. "I know it's been an exhausting process, but we're almost there. We have one more critical part to develop, and that's the executive summary."

Laura Chiang asked, "What about the cover letter and the table of contents?"

"The writing team is covering those. But you and James know the program design inside and out by now. I want you two to come up with a rough draft of the executive summary. And don't worry about getting it perfect. The writers will polish it after we get through reviewing what you've written."

She handed the two researchers a copy of the key elements list for the summary.

"Management wants these points emphasized. We have a great chance of winning this bid, so sell the client hard on our program design and health-care communications experience. Get them to believe we're the only ones who can do this project for them, and hook them on the benefits they'll receive."

"All that in two pages?" James Mullen asked.

"Go to three pages if you have to, but keep it short and to the point. Remember, you're writing for administrators, not the technical people at Everett."

Laura looked over the key elements list. "Give us a couple of days, and we'll see what we come up with."

Ms. Herras said, "I recommend that you take a look at our previous proposals for model executive summaries. This is your chance to tell the client why we're the best firm for the job. Keep the focus on what's most important to the client—their problem and our unique solution. Grab their attention and don't let go!"

*   *   *

Step 7: Front Matter and Executive Summary

Once you have written the program design and a draft of the proposal, they will be reviewed and revised by upper management. When the final content is approved, you will need to develop the front matter and executive summary to complete the proposal. The front matter includes the cover letter (also known as a transmittal letter), the title page, a proprietary notice, the table of contents, and a list of graphics (charts, photos, diagrams, etc.) that are included in the proposal.

The executive summary presents the main highlights of your proposal and gives you an opportunity to sell your solution and your company to the client. It is generally only one to two pages in length, although multivolume proposals may have longer executive summaries. In this chapter, we provide guidelines for creating these materials and present samples illustrating each one. A sample executive summary is provided in Appendix A.

The Front Matter

The client's first contact with your proposal will be the front matter pages. First impressions not only count, but they may determine whether the client bothers to read further. Many clients conduct first-round elimination of proposals based on only the cover letter and executive summary. It is well worth your time and effort to make sure your front matter helps you stay in the running for a contract.

Cover (Transmittal) Letter

A well-thought-out cover or transmittal letter can motivate the client to take a closer look at your proposal. The letter is usually bound into the proposal so that it is not accidentally lost or separated from the proposal itself. It should be signed by the senior officer on the project, the president, or CEO of your firm. The cover letter is less formal in tone than either the executive summary or the proposal and is considered a commitment from your senior executives to the client's officers. See Exhibit 6.1 for a sample cover letter.

EXHIBIT 6.1

Sample Cover Letter

Company Letterhead and Logo

November 15, 20—

Dr. Richard M. Pinsky
Executive Director
Everett Hospital, Inc.
1256 North Glendale Road
Glendale, GA 30366–3455

Dear Dr. Pinsky:

Integrated Medical Services, Inc., is proposing a complete solution for Everett Hospital's health-care interpreter network (HIN). Integrated Medical Services has the technical and software resources to ensure that the network requirements in the RFP are fully realized with a powerful, versatile architecture that meets and exceeds all technical specifications found in Everett Hospital's documentation. We also propose a partnership with World Medical Interpreters that will help Everett to access interpreters for any language needed, ensure quality patient care and efficient use of staff, ensure compliance with all government regulations, and position Everett as a premier health-care provider.

Integrated Medical Services offers a two-part solution to Everett's needs. Part I is the development of a voice/video interactive network linking Everett's health-care staff and patients with off-site interpreters such as World Medical Interpreters. The network will also link with all medical diagnostic and testing data, and with off-site medical experts and consultants. Part II involves implementation, training, and monitoring the network to ensure that all staff members know the system and that any technical problems are resolved quickly. Integrated Medical Systems will ensure the highest level of data security and will fully support both the network hardware and software after the project is completed.

Our firm has extensive experience in developing interactive voice/video networks; therefore, we feel that Everett's 18-month schedule is not only possible but comfortable. We have a database of successful architecture to serve as the foundation for the health-care interpreter network that Everett requires. Because of the highly technical nature of this proposal, we would welcome the opportunity to make a personal presentation to your management staff. This would enable your staff and ours to clarify any points before the final proposal evaluation.

Integrated Medical Services' proposal for the Health-care Interpreter Network Program (#621–853) and pricing are valid for 60 days. Mr. Hardin Tagore, an officer of Integrated Medical Services, is authorized to make all commitments presented in this proposal. Please direct all future communications to Ms. Nicolle Herras, who is managing the proposal process. Please include our proposal number in all future communications.

We look forward to working with you on the Health-care Interpreter Network Program.

Sincerely yours,

Hardin Tagore

Hardin Tagore
President

Nicolle Herras

Nicolle Herras
Vice President, Operations

Cover letters are a page or two in length and always contain the following information:

- Company name and address of the firm submitting the proposal, along with the address of the company's parent headquarters, if applicable
- A statement verifying that the person signing the proposal is fully authorized to make decisions about the terms and fees quoted in the document
- The name, title, and contact information of the person who is authorized to negotiate with the client on behalf of the company
- The names, titles, and contact information of those whom the client can contact for further information or clarification of the proposal
- Acknowledgment that the requirements and conditions of the RFP, along with any amendments, have been received, read, and accepted
- Any other information that you or your managers feel is necessary for the client to know

The body of the cover letter consists of at least three paragraphs. The opening paragraph provides a brief statement or summary of your marketing strategy or theme. Avoid the simple "thank you for allowing us to bid" statement. You need a stronger opening that emphasizes your product or service and why the client should choose your company over all the others.

The middle paragraph(s) offers a brief statement of the USP that will meet and exceed the client's needs. This is an opportunity to capture the client's interest in ways that go beyond the RFP. Also, use these middle paragraphs to explain any special research or other effort you took to identify critical requirements in the RFP or additional needs that may have been implied but not explicitly stated in the RFP.

The closing paragraph usually includes references to the RFP number (if one is given) and project name; length of time for which the proposal and its pricing are valid; a statement verifying that the signer of the letter is authorized to make commitments on behalf of your firm; and the name and address of the person in your firm who will act as the contact for future correspondence from the client. *Do not allow any other person in your company to talk with the client, unless you grant that person permission to do so.* You want to avoid any possible confusion, mixed messages, or miscommunications between your firm and the client.

Title Page

The title page format will vary according to each company—many firms have a company style they use. Exhibit 6.2 shows a sample of one firm's title page. In general, the page will contain the following:

- *"Response to requirements":* This phrase should be printed above the project name.
- *Client's name and address and the name of the person who signed the RFP:* Check with the client to verify where, to whom, and how to submit the proposal.
- *"Submitted by":* This line is printed above your firm's name, logo, and address.
- *Proposal number:* Refer to this number in your cover letter and request that the client refer to it in any correspondence. This adds a professional touch to your work and identifies each proposal in your computer files.
- *Controlled document number:* In highly sensitive proposals, you may wish to assign a controlled document number to keep track of each proposal copy. That is, if you distribute five copies, each one will have an assigned number (one through five) in addition to the proposal number. The controlled document number can be printed on a page with a holographic image or other image that cannot be reproduced. In this way, if anyone makes an unauthorized copy, it will be easy to spot the pirated version.
- *Date:* This must be the date the proposal is due, not the date you submit the proposal.
- *Master copy:* In some cases, you may want to designate one copy of the proposal as the master copy. This copy contains the original signed cover letter, while the other copies will have photocopies of the cover letter. If you designate a master copy, be sure to print MASTER COPY on the proposal cover and title page.

EXHIBIT 6.2

Sample Title Page

Response to Requirements
MEDICAL INTERPRETER NETWORK

Everett Hospital, Inc.
1256 North Glendale Road
Glendale, GA 30366–3455

Dr. Richard M. Pinsky
Executive Director

Proposal Submitted
by
Integrated Medical Systems, Inc.
455 Westlake Drive Suite 636
Chicago, IL 60644–1323

Everett Hospital Proposal No. 621–853

November 15, 20—

Proprietary Notice

Although not all proposals require a proprietary notice, it's a good rule of thumb to include one in any proposal you submit. The notice should appear at the bottom of each page, unless you have a non-disclosure statement. Basically, the notice states that the information contained in your proposal should not be released to anyone outside those who will evaluate it for the client. You need to protect your information from competitors and others who may use it without your permission and without giving you credit.

Remember, if you do not protect your work with the proprietary notice, your competitors can ask for and receive copies of your proposal under the federal Freedom of Information Act.

Because the requirements of each form vary, there is no generic proprietary notice form. Consult your legal department or a lawyer familiar with this area to help you draw up a notice that meets the needs of your company.

Table of Contents

The table of contents (TOC) is a list of all the major sections and subsections in your proposal and their page numbers. It helps the client find specific information quickly. TOCs vary widely depending on the length, complexity, and number of volumes of your proposal, but the following general rules apply to nearly all TOCs.

First, use a letter, Roman numeral, or numbered format for your headings (see Exhibit 6.3). If you have a short table of contents, you may want to list only the major headings. For a longer proposal, list only the first two levels of headings in the TOC.

Second, if you have more than one volume, include the TOCs from all the volumes in the first volume (see Exhibit 6.4). Subsequent volumes generally list only their own contents. However, you may prefer to include a brief table of contents for the other volumes as well. This approach may help the client keep the entire series in mind as they read each volume.

EXHIBIT 6.3
Sample Table of Contents—Single-Volume Proposal

A. Full Table of Contents

TABLE OF CONTENTS

COVER LETTER
EXECUTIVE SUMMARY

A.	OVERVIEW OF PROPOSED SOLUTION	A-1
	A.1 Assumptions and Implications	A-4
	A.2 Explanation of Integrated Network	A-6
	A.3 General Requirements	A-12
B.	TECHNICAL SECTION	B-1
	B.1 Overview of New Network	B-2
	B.2 Major Features	B-5
	B.3 Add-on Features	B-14

EXHIBIT 6.3 *(Continued)*

B.   Short Table of Contents

TABLE OF CONTENTS

List of Graphics

The list of graphics (charts, tables, photos, graphs, illustrations, etc.) follows the TOC and should be printed on a separate page or pages. You can either list each graphic in the order in which it appears, or separate each type of graphic into its own category (see Exhibit 6.5). If the graphics list is very short (two or three items), you can place it on the same page as your TOC.

EXHIBIT 6.4

Sample Table of Contents—Multiple-Volume Proposal

Volume 1: Technical Section

TABLE OF CONTENTS

Volume 2: Management Approach

TABLE OF CONTENTS

Volume 3: Time/Cost Estimates

TABLE OF CONTENTS

EXHIBIT 6.5

Sample List of Graphics and List of Tables

Graphics

FIGURES

		Page
Figure 1-1	Flow of Data from Terminal to Terminal	1-5
Figure 1-2	Flow of Data from Center to Center	1-6
Figure 1-3	Configuration of System Users	1-10
Figure 2-1	Proposed Project Management Steps	2-3
Figure 2-2	Project Team Organization Chart	2-6
Figure 3-1	Life Cycle of Software Development	3-2
Figure 3-2	Comparison of 6-Month and 12-Month Costs	3-5

Tables

TABLES

Table 1.1	Comparison of Program Features	1-3
Table 2.1	Project Manager's Duties	2-5
Table 3.1	Schedule for Project Completion	3-2
Table 3.2	Estimated Costs	3-4

Additional Front Matter

In addition to these items, there might be additional material you want to add to the front matter of your proposal. Common additions include a list of abbreviations, a compliance matrix and exceptions list, and an explanatory preface if your proposal is particularly complex:

- *Abbreviations list:* You may want to include an abbreviations list as a way to help the client understand the trade names, acronyms, and buzzwords unique to your company or business. Such a list is generally part of your boilerplate files and is placed after the list of graphics in your proposal.
- *Compliance matrix and exceptions list:* Many government RFPs require a compliance matrix to show that you have met the major requirements and specifications in the RFP. If you

cannot be compliant in all areas, you should explain each exception. For example, you may have a product or service that makes one or two requirements unnecessary. By explaining your reasons, you have a chance to highlight certain features of your product or service.

- *"How to read this proposal"*: If your proposal is complex and difficult to follow, you may want to provide a preface to help readers find their way through the text.

In addition to these features, some RFPs may require you to establish a bond (bid check, performance bond, payment bond) when you submit the proposal. Others may require you to sign a statement in which you agree to buy a certain percentage of goods manufactured in the United States for the supplies used in your project work. Or they may require that you use organic, biodegradable, or nontoxic materials in your work and make every effort to reduce your carbon footprint.

The Executive Summary

The executive summary is primarily focused on the key features of your unique solution and its benefits, and includes a brief description of how you will accomplish the work. Keep in mind that you are writing for executives, not technical staff, so concentrate on the business reasons for why the client should choose your firm over your competitors. (See Appendix A for a sample executive summary.) In addition to providing the main points of your program design, you can use the executive summary to do the following:

- Demonstrate your grasp of the client's problem
- Market your solution and its benefits and their advantages over what competitors might offer
- Translate complex technical concepts, products, or processes into readily understandable terms
- Present pertinent information not requested in the RFP
- Educate the client about your firm and its products, staff, and resources
- Reinforce how the client will benefit by choosing your firm to do the job

The executive summary is your most effective and important sales and marketing piece. It deserves all the effort and attention you put into it. Remember, clients often use the executive summary as their initial screening process. So keep your focus on the results, benefits, and value for price rather than on the details of how you will do the work.

Who Reads the Executive Summary?

Although the executive summary is read by a wide range of people in the client's organization, your main audience is the top executive or executive group with the authority to award the contract. This person or group reads all of the executive summaries in order to grasp the major strengths, weaknesses, and unique features of each proposal. Your executive summary is an opportunity to market your solution and your firm.

The executive summary is also read by other members of the evaluation staff to gain an overview of your proposal before they examine its more detailed sections. In this way, staff members have a context for judging your program design and will better understand your technical approach, management plan, and time/cost estimates. Whether you also include the pricing strategy in the executive summary is a matter of judgment. You will have to determine in each case whether there is some advantage to doing so.

The executive summary is designed to answer a progressive series of questions:

1. What is your solution or approach to the problem?
2. Why was that solution or approach chosen and how did you arrive at it?
3. What are the key elements of the solution or approach (usually, the technical aspects)?
4. What are the main benefits to the client?
5. Are there any exceptions taken to the RFP requirements or any problem areas that need to be addressed?
6. How will the project be managed and what are the time/cost estimates?
7. What happens after the project is finished?
8. Who is your firm and why do you believe you can do the job?

Outline of the Executive Summary

Although some RFPs include guidelines for developing the executive summary, many do not. Those that do include guidelines may ask you to provide a brief description or outline of the proposed solution and include any areas of concern that need to be addressed. However, you must still interpret what is meant by "brief description or outline" and "any areas of concern that need to be addressed." The client may state that no pricing or time/cost estimates should be included. On the other hand, they may require an overview of your major time/cost estimates.

In general, executive summaries contain some or all of the following topics, which are discussed in more detail below:

- Introduction
- Program design
- Technical approach
- Project management plan
- Implementation, monitoring, maintenance
- Training
- Time/cost
- Company profile
- Future products or services

You may not need to include all these topics for every one of the executive summaries you write. For example, on some projects you may not be involved with implementation, monitoring, or maintenance, or you may not be required to train the client's workforce.

Introduction

By the time you are ready to write the executive summary, you should know the client and the client's problem so well that you can put yourself in the decision maker's shoes and ask, "What would I want to know from this executive summary? What would grab my attention and keep me reading?" Would you want to wade through an extensive description of the bidder's company, how fantastic their products or services are, and their qualifications? Or would you want to know what the bidder is going to do for you? The introduction should grab the readers' attention by focusing on what is important to them—a solution to their problem and the benefits that solution will provide.

Opening Paragraphs

Your first few paragraphs must start off marketing your solution. Many companies make the mistake of launching into a detailed profile of their firm and its capabilities, reciting a list of similar projects they completed successfully. The client cares more about their own immediate problems than about your past successes.

The first paragraphs must accomplish the following three goals:

- Restate the client's primary problem or goal and set the tone for the proposal
- Present your firm's solution to the problem or your firm's promise to meet the goal
- Establish the proposal theme, which is reinforced throughout each section

Tell the client what will be gained by awarding you the job—not what will be lost if they don't hire you. Positive selling is far more powerful and effective than negative selling. The sample paragraphs below illustrate a winning proposal opening:

> Everett Hospital's goal of providing interpreters for all of its non-English-speaking patients requires a sophisticated network of voice/video communications that goes beyond the usual communications network. As stated in the RFP, this network must ensure prompt, reliable interpretive services for over 60 different languages; ensure effective immediate and follow-up care for patients; facilitate efficient use of health-care staff; and fully satisfy all government regulations. The network must also be mobile, easy to operate, and fully supported by technical and staff training personnel. In addition to the RFP requirements, we also see the need for Everett Hospital to partner with a major interpretive services provider, such as World Medical Interpreters, to guarantee that Everett will have quick, easy access to all the languages that patients speak.

Our solution will provide Everett Hospital not only with the health-care interpreter services it needs but also with an effective partner to make the most of the interpreter services available to the hospital through a communications network. This strategy will position the hospital to provide high-quality care for its diverse population, to add additional languages to the network as they are needed, to provide added incentives to attract the best health-care professionals to its facilities, and to expand the interpreter network to Everett's satellite facilities in the future.

It is our intention in this proposal to describe how we will accomplish these goals and to demonstrate our firm's commitment to help Everett Hospital achieve its objectives of providing superior health care to patients and becoming one of the premier health-care facilities in the state.

These opening paragraphs draw the client into the proposal and promise a solution that other bidders, it is hoped, will be unable to match or surpass. The paragraphs also point out a new requirement that the original RFP did not contain but that may be critical to the client's success and future growth. Right away, the reader is hooked and eager to turn the page to find out more.

Program Design

While the introduction announces the solution to the client's problem, this section of the executive summary states briefly how and why you chose this particular solution. You need to show that you understand not only what is requested in the RFP but also the problems associated with finding the right answers. You can present your case in terms of trade-offs, that is, the benefits and costs of each option. This section should show the client why your solution offers the best cost/benefit ratio.

For instance, in the sample case, Integrated Medical Systems is proposing to set up a partnership between Everett Hospital and World Medical Interpreters. This part of the solution will increase Everett's upfront costs and add to the complexity of the voice/video system they need. However, Integrated Medical Systems could emphasize the obvious trade-off: the ability to quickly reach an interpreter for any language at any time of the day or night. The cost/benefit ratio is strongly in Everett's favor. Integrated Medical Systems could point out why *not* adopting this part of the solution could cost the hospital far more in terms of liability than they will spend on the partnership and new system.

Technical Approach

The technical approach section of the executive summary answers the question, "What are the key elements of the solution?" Generally, you will follow the outline or list of requirements as they are presented in the RFP. After reading this part, the client should have a good grasp of your solution and how well you have responded to the RFP requirements.

Always keep in mind that you are writing for a largely nontechnical audience. Top management decision makers seldom have the expertise to understand the precise technical aspects of the product or service proposed. Make sure that you explain or define key terms and keep all technical jargon and details to a minimum. For example, Everett Hospital administrators may not be able to follow a detailed discussion of the architecture of the voice/video call system, but they would understand a description of its features and how it would enable them to achieve their goals.

Clients should find all the essential information they require in the executive summary. In general, avoid referring the reader to the technical section or to an appendix in the proposal. Not only will you break the reader's focus, but some RFPs actually label this tactic as "nonresponsive to the requirements." If the client needs more information, you can designate one person on your staff to answer their questions.

Project Management Plan

The more complex or technical the project, the more important a solid management plan becomes. Like the technical approach portion, this part of the executive summary should be a brief description of the management plan. In this section, you need to answer the following questions:

- How will the project be managed?
- Who will be on the project team?
- What responsibilities will each member assume?

- What will be the proposed schedule?
- How will your firm, the client, and any subcontractors work together?

You can include a brief work schedule and go into slightly more detail in the time/cost portion. Or, if the RFP states that no cost information should be included, you can present your work schedule plan in greater detail here. Be sure to state clearly who will be supervising which tasks of the project. If you are using a joint consultant/client management team, clarify which responsibilities will be delegated to which personnel and who will be the contact person for both parties.

Implementation, Monitoring, and Maintenance

When writing this section, you are answering the question, "What happens after the project is finished?" The client will want to know how you will help to introduce the product or service to their firm and how you will support your work once the final payment has been made. Remember: strong customer service can be the value-added feature that helps you stand out from the competition. In many instances, this feature carries greater weight than the cost component when a client is making a final decision.

Today, the demand for quality implementation, monitoring, and maintenance services is increasing. This trend is occurring for several reasons.

First, clients must determine their return on investment based not only on initial costs but on implementation and maintenance expenses as well. If the initial price is a bargain but the cost of maintaining a product or service over time is high, the clients haven't received the best value for their money.

Second, the implementation, monitoring, and maintenance services are particularly critical when the following conditions apply:

- When companies win jobs in areas where they do not have adequately trained maintenance personnel
- When companies bid products that have not been fully tested
- When companies find themselves short of staff because of rapid growth, merger, or acquisition

Finally, companies are trying to get increased value for the money they spend. As a result, client service and support has become an even more important factor in choosing suppliers than it used to be.

Many clients, to protect themselves, include penalty clauses if their new system is down for more than a specified amount of time or if client personnel find the new product, service, or process too difficult, cumbersome, or inefficient to use. In most cases, you may not be able to issue a warranty on many of the services you provide to clients. As a result, a quality implementation, monitoring, and maintenance plan can ensure the client's satisfaction with your work after you have completed the initial project.

Education and Training

The management plan should include a description of all staff education and training needed for the project. The client must be confident that your firm can provide their workers with the knowledge and skills they need to use the new software, equipment, or procedures you develop. This section of the executive summary should serve as a brief overview of your training department or function and should include basic information on the following subjects:

- Why education and training sessions are required for the project and which staff members will need this service
- Members of your training staff and their qualifications
- Types of instruction you provide (computer-assisted, interactive video, lecture, self-learning)
- Provisions for training at your facility or on-site at the client's location
- An overview of how long the training will take and how much it will cost
- Follow-up training for those who require it (new employees, transferred staff, etc.)

If you present a comprehensive, well-written overview of your education and training capabilities, you send a message to the client that your company knows what it takes to develop a successful solution. You also appear to be a well-organized and established firm capable of backing up your work.

Time/Cost

The time/cost section of the executive summary can be one of the most persuasive arguments for choosing your firm. *However, pay close attention to the requirements in the RFP regarding time/cost information.* Some RFPs specifically request that pricing be omitted because it may influence a selection that should be based on program design or some other feature. Others may require that you include how you calculate your costs and explain any special discounts or pricing you might be offering.

If the RFP you are responding to does not explicitly exclude pricing information, you have been given a good opportunity to sell your firm in this section. You can provide a summary of your schedule and costs and explain briefly any special conditions, exceptions, additions, or discounts that were involved in developing the final estimates. You can also use the pricing summary to mention any special terms and conditions in the RFP, explain any optional products or services not requested in the RFP, and justify any exceptions to RFP requirements. You should also use this section to highlight any price/value advantages you may have over your competition (special supplier arrangements, shipping discounts, proprietary information, software licenses, and the like).

A description of your schedule should include a summary of the milestones for all major tasks in the project. All dates assigned to the schedule should match the dates listed in the RFP. You don't need a detailed breakdown of tasks at this point. You want to give the client an overview of how the project will be accomplished, not a detailed timetable for each step. This section allows the client to evaluate whether you understand their time frame for the project and whether your work estimates are realistic.

The time/cost section also offers you an opportunity to present alternative schedules and cost structures. You may have developed two or three time/cost estimates based on what the client wants done and how quickly it needs to be accomplished. For example, some clients may award more evaluation points to firms that offer the fastest installation time.

You can also explain any deviations from the RFP— for example, why you are not bidding on a portion of the RFP or what additions to the RFP requirements you believe are necessary. For instance, you may see a need to add equipment or staff to the project that the client did not anticipate.

Even if your estimated costs are higher than those of your competitors, your firm won't automatically be eliminated from the bidding—provided you can justify those costs. The price/value trade-offs have to make sense to the client before they will accept your solution.

Your Company Profile

The company profile gives you an opportunity to introduce your company and highlight its unique resources and capabilities. If the client has worked with your firm previously, this part of the summary gives you an opportunity to update the client on your firm's current resources and strengths. This can be particularly important if your firm has grown considerably or changed its focus in the past few years.

Your company profile should include at least the following information:

- When the company was founded and a statement of its mission or objectives
- A brief history of the company's development and contributions to the industry
- Company organization and its features and benefits
- Types of equipment/products/services you provide
- Locations of headquarters and divisions or affiliates, and number of employees
- References—the most important clients served and the projects completed for them

In this part of the executive summary, it is often useful to include an organization chart of departments or divisions and top management (president/CEO, vice presidents, executive directors, etc.) as well as a map showing your firm's locations and affiliates. These graphics enable the reader to grasp your company's organization and size at a glance.

After reading this section, the client should have a solid understanding of who and what your firm is and where the client's project will be placed in your organization.

Future Products and Other Elements

Like the time/cost section, this part of the executive summary is optional and gives you the chance to comment on current or late-breaking technology or other events related to the client's problems and opportunities. If appropriate, you may wish to include a final section outlining what you believe to be future spinoffs or directions the company could take based on the current proposed project. Or you may wish to share information on the direction of future technology that relates to a product, service, or process you are providing. This information shows the client that they are buying into something that will help them stay abreast or even ahead of their changing markets. For example, you may know of new alternative energy sources that might help power the production machinery that you are designing for the client.

This part of the executive summary can demonstrate your company's ability to keep pace with current changes in technology, marketing, and resources. The message you give the client is that your firm has financial, technical, and management resources and strengths that may not be obvious in other parts of your proposal.

Common Errors

Look over the following list of common errors that companies make in writing the executive summary. Check your past proposals or the rough draft of your current executive summary to make sure that you have not made any of these common mistakes:

- *Forgetting who the primary audience is:* Top management—not technical personnel or line managers—read the executive summary; some managers may read *only* the summary and leave the rest of the proposal to technical personnel and others to evaluate.
- *Writing an opening paragraph that is too general and/or too negative:* Vague writing or fear tactics are not good selling tools.
- *Going into too much detail regarding how results will be achieved:* Remember, the client's top management are interested primarily in the solution to their problems and not the details about every step in the process.

- *Using too many technical terms or jargon:* Readers of the executive summary often are not experts in the technical aspects of your solution.
- *Including too many graphics or additional materials:* Keep it simple; use only the graphics that are absolutely necessary to clarify or support your text (e.g., organization charts, flow charts).

In addition, be sure not to insert material that the RFP expressly states should *not* be included (e.g., scheduling or pricing information, supporting documents, references to other sections or parts of the proposal).

EXECUTIVE SUMMARY CHECKLIST

The executive summary of your proposal serves as your public relations, marketing, and sales presentation. The time and effort you spend on this section is an important investment not only in the current job you are bidding but for future business as well.

- ❑ Did you examine the RFP carefully to determine what should or should not be included in the executive summary?
- ❑ Do you know the readers' levels of knowledge and expertise?
- ❑ Is the executive summary focused on results, not details?
- ❑ Do your opening paragraphs focus on the client's problems and your solution/benefits and establish the proposal theme?
- ❑ In the program design section, did you briefly explain how and why you developed your solution?
- ❑ Did you explain the technical aspects by emphasizing benefits and minimizing technical jargon and details?
- ❑ If presenting the project management plan, did you include the following?
  - ❑ How the project will be managed?
  - ❑ Who will be on the project team?
  - ❑ What are the responsibilities of each project team member?
  - ❑ What is the proposed work schedule?
  - ❑ How your firm and the client will interact?
- ❑ Did you emphasize customer service in your implementation, monitoring, and maintenance section?

❑   Did you include the following in your education and training section?
   ❑   Brief overview of your training department
   ❑   Training staff
   ❑   Types of instruction you use
   ❑   Description of in-house and client site training facilities
   ❑   Follow-up training procedures
❑   If the time/cost section is included, did you:
   ❑   Mention any special terms and conditions?
   ❑   Explain any optional products, equipment, or services not requested in the RFP?
   ❑   Justify exceptions to the RFP?
   ❑   Highlight price/value advantages you have over your competition?
   ❑   Offer alternative time schedules and cost estimates?
❑   Have you used the company profile to include at least the following:
   ❑   Company history and primary mission
   ❑   Brief description of your firm's contributions to industry
   ❑   Equipment/products/services you offer
   ❑   Company organization and its features and benefits
   ❑   Number and location of facilities or affiliates and number of employees
   ❑   Client references and completed projects
❑   Did you mention any future product or other essential information?
❑   Did you make sure that all the graphics included are necessary in your proposal?

7

Producing Your Proposal

"James, can you give me a hand with this section?" Laura asked.

James Mullen wheeled his chair over to Laura's desk and peered at her screen. "What's the problem?"

"I can't figure out a way to display this call routing data. I have to show the client how their call traffic might look in three years."

"Why not show it in two comparison diagrams?"

"How? There are too many parts to this."

"No, no, here." James used Laura's mouse to log on to the company server. "We've got a graphics file for showing call routing data over time. Here, call up File MS.23. I used it last month for the Fournier voice/video network we did."

Laura glanced over the diagrams and smiled. "This should show them exactly what we're talking about in the proposal. Thanks! I have to get this section finished for the production coordinator by tomorrow. Ms. Herras wants this for the final draft on Friday—it's going to the executive committee for review."

"I know. Paula over in Finance said they have two teams working on the time and cost estimates to get them done."

Laura sat back, shaking her head. "We started this proposal weeks ago, and it's still turning into a mashup."

*   *   *

Step 8: Proposal Production

Once you have all the sections of the proposal complete, you can begin the production stage to put the entire proposal together. The proposal manager may coordinate this effort or may turn the proposal drafts over to a production supervisor to have the work done. Production usually occurs in the following order:

1. Rough drafts of all sections and graphics are given to the production team.
2. The final proposal design and production budget are developed and approved. The production budget is generally part of the original budget for proposal development.
3. A complete document is assembled and submitted to top management for review.
4. All changes are inserted into the document; it is given a final edit, proofread, and then printed. Depending on the proposal, steps 3 and 4 may be repeated several times before a final document is approved.
5. Top management and all team members read the proposal in a final review.
6. Any further corrections, changes, or additions are made.
7. The document is prepared usually in both electronic and printed form and delivered or given as a formal presentation to the client's top management.

Because you generally have limited time when you reach this stage, planning is critical. All the various elements of the proposal—title page, table of contents and list of graphics and tables, cover letter, executive summary, body of the proposal, appendixes, and any other supporting material—must be ushered through production to finished product. Countless decisions must be made along the way: What typeface and style of graphics should be used? Will the proposal be presented in person, by DVD or other electronic media, or in printed form only? If printed, what type of paper, cover, and binding should be used? How will last-minute changes be made? What happens if a graphic, appendix, or table needs to be added or deleted?

All these decisions, and the production tasks involved, can be made easier by creating a production control schedule to keep track of each step in the process. Exhibit 7.1 shows an example of the production form similar to those used by many companies. The production coordinator can see at a glance what needs to be done, when it is due, and who has primary responsibility.

Production Guidelines

With today's publishing software, even a one-person firm can produce high-quality, professional-looking proposals at a reasonable cost. The real trick is in knowing how to use design, layout, type styles, and graphics to your best advantage. The right presentation of your data can make it easier for the client to appreciate your grasp of their situation and to understand your proposed solutions.

This chapter focuses on helping you learn the basics of producing a proposal, particularly using graphics and tables, to give you the best chance at winning the contract. These principles hold true whether you produce your proposals in-house or hire a designer or printer to do them for you.

Know Your Client

The rule "know your client" is as true for the production side of proposal writing as it is for the development side. Is the client known for being conservative, innovative, middle of the road? Examine client publications for clues to their preferences in production. Does the client use full-color displays in its publications? Or does

EXHIBIT 7.1
Proposal Production Schedule

RFP: 621–853 Everett Hospital													Date: 9/27/20—
Task	10/1	10/5	10/6	10/10	10/11	10/12	10/13	10/15	10/18	10/21	10/22	10/25	Responsibilities and Comments
First draft	X												
• Executive summary—edit		X											Mullen and Chiang
• Cover letter—edit		X	X	X									VP Herras
• Proposal chapters—edit					X								Proposal team
• Appendixes—edit					X								Proposal team
• Illustrations						X							Production department
• Review first draft						X							VP Herras and VP Warner
Final draft													
• Executive summary							X						VP Herras and Mr. Tagore
• Cover letter								X					VP Herras
• Proposal chapters								X	X	X			Executive committee
• Appendixes										X			Proposal team
• Illustrations										X			Production department
Production													Production department
• Binders											X		S. Uhland
Sign-off											X		VP Herras, Mr. Tagore, & executive committee
Delivery												X	ENI delivery service

the client seem attracted to more conservative displays and colors? Even if your firm has a standard format for creating a proposal, you can and should customize the document for the client.

Get to know the "personality" or style of the client firm and tailor your production preparation accordingly. One firm jeopardized its proposal by opting for more abstract graphics and cover designs. The client was a fairly conservative manufacturing company and had the impression that the proposal team didn't really understand the nature of the manufacturing business. Remember, images often speak louder than words.

A clash between the proposal's style and the client's preferred style puts needless obstacles in your path. Take the time to do a little research on the client's expectations and preferences. This is not to say that you shouldn't take chances by designing a more interesting cover or inserting a few artistic graphics. Just be sure that the client is likely to be pleasantly surprised by them and not left wondering for whom the proposal was developed.

Format—Swipe Files and Boilerplates

Most firms have an established format for their proposals. Proposal writers simply follow the format to create the title page, table of contents, executive summary, headings and divisions of each section, and appendixes. Some firms may use a variety of formats, depending on the type of project they are bidding on.

In many instances, writers do not have to create all the elements of a proposal. Items such as contracts, time/cost sections, company qualifications, list of work done for previous clients, and staff résumés can be placed in computer swipe files or be part of the company boilerplates. This information can then be called up and inserted into the document at the appropriate places. Shortcuts like these make it easier to assemble a proposal, particularly when time is critical and the production schedule is short. Make sure the stored material is updated periodically to keep it current.

Criteria for Using Graphics instead of Words

Most people are familiar with tables, charts, and graphs; they are a common staple of reports, print media, Web articles, blogs, and television news. But few people understand *why* particular data are shown using particular kinds of tables, charts, or graphs. In this section, we review the purpose of the most common graphic formats and which types of data are best displayed using each one.

In determining when to use words and when to use tables and other graphics, keep the following criteria in mind as you are developing drafts of your proposal sections. Tables, charts, and graphs are better than words when:

- You need to reinforce the facts in your text with supporting images or graphics.
- You need to describe complex technical or physical processes. How does cocaine affect the human body? How does an assembly line work? How will changes in an inner-city design affect traffic flow in and around the area?
- You have complex numerical or statistical data to convey. For example, you may need to summarize the results of public opinion surveys on the client's new product offerings. Or you need to present the results of drug rehabilitation treatment programs for 50 clinics. One table or chart can save you a page or two of text and present the data in a form the reader can grasp far more quickly and easily.
- You are describing something that requires the reader to form a mental image in order to understand it. A city plan, the interior of a building, the inner workings of a cell or virus—all these can be described verbally but are far clearer when presented in an illustration. A picture gives the reader a visual reference for your text.
- You want to present information in a form the reader will be able to recall easily. In general, most people remember visual images better than they do words. If you are talking about the four critical elements of top-quality software, for example, you might use a graph such as the one shown in Exhibit 7.2, to present the information visually.

As you develop your draft proposal, note in the margins where you think tables, charts, or other graphics will be needed.

EXHIBIT 7.2

Visual Presentation of Text Information

Four Elements of Excellent Software

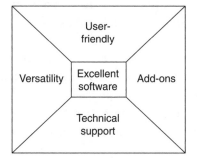

Using Tables and Graphics Effectively

There are two principles governing the use of tables and graphic materials:

1. *Visual materials must be essential to your proposal and not used to conceal a lack of content.* Graphics and tables must provide important information and not be used simply to fill out the page or to impress the client.
2. *Visual materials must support and clarify the text, not stand in place of it.* Graphics and tables must be properly labeled, inserted in the right place, and explained or interpreted in the text. You cannot assume that the reader will understand what a graph, diagram, or photo represents. The complex structure of a voice/video call routing network, for example, must have some type of accompanying caption or text explaining its main features.

Types of Tables and Graphics

There are six basic forms to illustrate information in your proposal: tables, pie or circle graphs, bar charts, line graphs, organization and flow charts, and pictures or symbols. Exhibits 7.3 through 7.8 provide examples of all six types of graphics. The one you choose depends on the information you have to display and the point you are trying to make.

For example, suppose you are examining changes in the characteristics of drug users who enroll in drug treatment programs. You want to compare 2004 and 2009 data on this topic. The paragraph in your rough draft might read as follows:

> From 2004 to 2009, the age group of drug users enrolling in drug treatment programs changed considerably. In 2004 those aged 13 to 18 years comprised 42 percent of all enrollees, those aged 19 to 29 comprised 21 percent, those aged 30 to 45 comprised 15 percent, and those over 45 comprised 22 percent. In 2009, these figures had shifted dramatically. Enrollees 13 to 18 years of age represented only 35 percent of all enrollees, the 19 to 29 age group increased to 43 percent, the 30 to 45 age group accounted for only 12 percent, and the over 45 age group represented only 10 percent of the total.

These are a lot of data for the reader to absorb. You can arrange the information in a table to help the reader see the figures at a glance (see Exhibit 7.3). Although this method presents the information in a convenient form, it offers little visual interpretation of the data to assist the reader in understanding what they may mean.

EXHIBIT 7.3
Sample Table

Table 1.1 – Drug Users in Treatment Groups—2004 to 2009

| | Percent of total | |
Age group	2004	2009
13–18	42%	35%
19–29	21%	43%
30–45	15%	12%
45+	22%	10%

Suppose you wanted to present the information more graphically to underscore a point about the success of enrolling members of the 19- to 29-year-old age group in drug treatment programs. A bar chart would show the reader in which group drug use declined the most (see Exhibit 7.4A).

On the other hand, suppose you wanted to show that the 19- to 29-year-old age group accounts for an increasing percentage of the total population of drug treatment users. A pie or circle chart would be the best choice to illustrate your point (see Exhibit 7.4B). Each group is represented by a wedge in the circle. This format enables the reader to grasp quickly how much the 19- to 29-year-old age group has increased in five years.

If you want to depict changes in the various age groups over time, you would use a line graph, which depicts the steady progression of change over a fixed period of time (see Exhibit 7.4C). You can explain in your text why the upsurge in enrollment of 19- to 29-year-olds occurred and why enrollment of 13- to 18-year-olds declined.

Finally, you can use symbols to show changes in group enrollment to give the reader a better grasp of how large the increases and decreases are in a more dramatic way. (See Exhibit 7.4D).

In your text, you can discuss the implications of the data shown in any chart or graph. For example, people aged 19 to 29 who enroll in drug treatment programs are likely to have small children. As a result, they will need child support services—which will be critical to the success of the drug treatment program. Those in older age categories are less likely to have as many infants and small children and will require different types of services.

Common Errors

The guidelines below can help you avoid the most common mistakes proposal writers make when using graphics and tables. The two most common errors are (1) using too many graphics and tables and (2) not explaining them well enough.

1. *Use only the graphics essential to the proposal text.* Unfortunately, many proposal developers believe that if a few graphics are good, more are better. They use so many charts, tables, and

EXHIBIT 7.4 A–D
Graphic Presentation of Tabular Data

A. Bar Chart

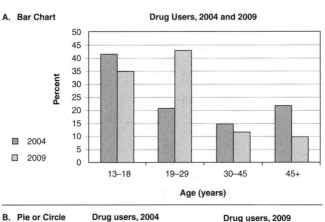

B. Pie or Circle Graph

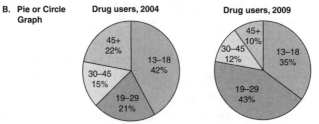

C. Line Graph

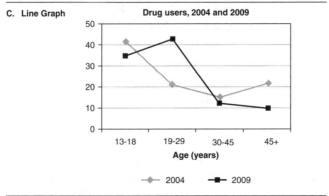

D. Symbol Chart

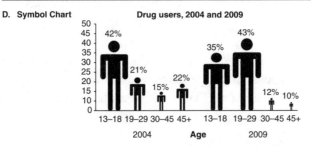

graphs that they overwhelm the body of the text. Use only those graphics that emphasize a point, explain key facts in the text, or help the reader remember essential information.

2. *Make sure all your graphics and tables are designed to the same scale.* Avoid broad discrepancies in size between one graphic and another—for example, a line graph that takes up a quarter page and a circle chart that takes up a full page. Use the same scale to create all charts.

3. *Be sure that the terms you use in the graphic or table are the same terms used in the text.* This point is particularly critical when developing proposals for international clients. If you talk about kilometers in the text, don't use miles in the table. If you are copying the graphic from another source, adapt the terms so they are consistent with your text (for example, change Celsius to Fahrenheit).

4. *Use your best judgment when constructing three-dimensional (3-D) charts.* The general rule of thumb is to make it easier— not harder—for the reader to grasp the information presented in the graphic. Three-dimensional circle charts are fine, but line charts in 3-D can be confusing to the eye. You don't want your graphics to confuse, distract, or frustrate your client.

5. *Mention the number and name of the graphic or table in the text as close to the actual graphic or table as possible.* Let the reader know that the graphic exists early in the relevant paragraph. Don't wait until the next page to mention it.

6. *Be consistent with the format you use to set up tables, charts, and graphs.* If your company has an established format for graphics and tables, follow it closely. Otherwise, create a format and make sure every table and graph is set up in the same style. This not only helps to eliminate confusion but it makes your data easier to follow or compare from one illustration or table to the next.

7. *Number all tables and graphics consecutively throughout your proposal.* Again, your company may have an established style for numbering tables and illustrations (e.g., Table 1, Table A, Table 1.1, Figure 1.1, Exhibit II, and so on). If there is no established system, set one up and use it throughout the proposal. In general, don't mix tables and figures when numbering sequentially. For example, number tables Table 1, Table 2, and

so on, and number figures Figure 1, Figure 2, and so on. In your list of graphics and tables in your front matter, list the tables separately from the figures or exhibits.

8. *Cite your source for the information in each table or graphic.* If you used government or private research other than your own, cite the source in a footnote at the bottom of the table or graphic. Find out if you need permission to use the information or if there are other restrictions on usage.

Interpreting Tables and Graphics

It is not enough to insert graphics into your proposal. Your readers need to know what the graphics mean, and *you* must interpret the data for them. For the data on groups enrolling in drug treatment programs, for example, don't merely restate the figures in the text. Tell the readers why the changes are meaningful or important. Are treatment programs for the 30 and above age groups declining, receiving fewer referrals, failing the enrollees, or graduating more people than they enroll? Does the increase in the 19 to 29 age group represent the success of a drug treatment outreach program, an increase in funding for programs, better reporting methods, or simply a larger percentage of the population reaching that age group?

You must also explain how the data directly affect the client's products or services. If the client is involved in providing drug treatment programs, for instance, does the data suggest further opportunities for outreach? Will the client need to expand the programs or reduce them, change the age focus, or coordinate with other agencies? Your job is to interpret the facts and figures you present to help the client clearly understand what benefits or challenges the data represent to them.

Designing Tables and Graphics

Although each form of table and graphic has its own requirements, there are a few general guidelines for designing effective graphics:

- *All graphics and tables should be referred to in the text by number and title.* This enables the reader to grasp quickly the main point of the graphic or table and easily find it in the proposal. The client can then refer back and forth between the text and graphic or table.

- *All elements of the graphic or table should be properly labeled.* In a line chart, for example, label all lines clearly so that the reader can easily distinguish among them. In a diagram or flow chart, label all parts and clearly indicate the direction of the process or chart.
- *Keep the number of colors or patterns to a minimum in any one graphic or table.* Too many colors or patterns are confusing to the eye and obscure your data. The client will stop reading in frustration.
- *If you use keys, legends, or any other notes, do not obscure any part of the graphic.* Notes containing explanations or source citations should be placed below the graphic or in a position that does not block part of the image or table.
- *Cite the source of your data below the graphic or table.* Unless you have developed the data yourself, you will need to cite the source for your facts and figures.

Tables—Showing and Comparing Numbers

Tables are particularly useful for displaying numbers in columns. They have the added advantages of being easy to produce and easy to change.

- A table has at least two columns and two rows, with headings at the top of each column to indicate what the figures or information in the table represents.
- If the table contains a long series of items, make the table easier to read by arranging the data into groups of two, three, or four lines or by highlighting every other line. If the table is particularly long or complex, you can also use vertical or horizontal lines to separate columns and rows of information into a more readable format.
- Use single line spaces between rows of numbers within tables. Use double line spaces between groups of data and between the column headings and the first row of figures or data.
- All figures in a table should be aligned on the right. Commas, decimal points, dollar or percentage signs, and other symbols are aligned vertically. In most cases, numbers should be rounded to the nearest hundredth; that is, they should not extend further than two places to the right of the decimal point.

The examples in Exhibit 7.5 A–C show some of the ways that tables can be prepared.

EXHIBIT 7.5 A–C

Sample Tables

A. Solid Waste Generation—1980–2007 (millions of tons/year)

Materials	1980	1990	2000	2005	2007
Paper and paperboard	36.4%	35.4%	36.7%	33.9%	32.7%
Glass	10	6.4	5.3	5.3	5.3
Metals	10.2	8.1	7.9	8	8.2
Plastics	4.5	8.3	10.7	11.7	12.1
Rubber and leather	2.8	2.8	2.8	2.9	2.9
Textiles	1.7	2.8	3.9	4.5	4.7
Wood	4.6	6	5.5	5.6	5.6
Other	1.7	1.6	1.7	1.7	1.7
Food wastes	8.6	10.1	11.2	12.1	12.5
Yard wastes	18.1	17.1	12.8	12.8	12.8
Other wastes	1.5	1.4	1.5	1.5	1.5
Totals	100%	100%	100%	100%	100%

Source: *Statistical Abstract of the U.S—2010*

B. Threatened and Endangered Species in the World, 2009

Category	Endangered U.S.	Endangered Foreign	Threatened U.S.	Threatened Foreign	Species Total
Mammals	69	256	13	20	358
Birds	75	179	15	6	275
Reptiles	13	66	24	16	119
Amphibians	14	8	11	1	34
Fishes	74	11	65	1	151
Snails	24	1	11	0	36
Clams	62	2	8	0	72
Crustaceans	19	0	3	0	22
Insects	47	4	10	0	61
Plants	600	1	146	2	749
Total	997	528	306	46	1,877

Source: U.S. Fish and Wildlife Service

C. Murder by Type of Weapon, 2008

Region	Firearms	Cutting weapons	Other	Personal[1]	Total[2]
Northeast	62.8	18.1	14.4	4.7	100.0
Midwest	68.6	10.1	15.2	6.1	100.0
South	67.9	12.5	13.5	6.1	100.0
West	66.5	14.4	12.2	6.9	100.0

[1]   Hands, feet, etc.; includes pushed as a personal weapon.
[2]   Because of rounding, the percentages may not add to 100.0.

Source: *Crime in the United States, 2008*. U.S. Department of Justice, FBI, September, 2009

Bar Charts—Showing Relationships among Groups

Bar or column charts depict relationships among groups of information, such as the number of kilowatts of energy produced in different states over the past 10 years. Bars can be arranged vertically or horizontally. Most computer spreadsheets and graphics programs can be used to create these charts easily.

Stack bar charts show data in segments of a bar and compare one segmented bar to another. These types of bar charts must be clearly labeled to avoid confusing the reader. Generally, limit the number of segments per bar to five or fewer and use colors that are not similar to one another to distinguish each segment. Avoid using similar shades of green, for example. Instead use green, yellow, and blue to mark segments in a stack.

When making a bar chart, be sure to label each bar clearly. Avoid creating labels in such a way that the reader has to rotate the page to read the information. Exhibit 7.6A–B shows the preferred way to construct these charts.

Circle Graphs—Showing Relationship to the Whole

Circle graphs are particularly useful when you want to show the relative sizes of groups compared to the whole. Circle graphs show the reader at a glance the proportion of each slice to other slices and to the whole. In general, limit the number of segments to ten or fewer. If you try to pack too many segments into the circle, it will be difficult to distinguish one segment from another. Spreadsheet and graphic computer programs can be used to construct circle graphs quickly.

Circle graphs can also be used to show progressive changes over time and to compare the changes in each segment as well as in the whole. Exhibit 7.7 A–C demonstrates the different uses of circle graphs.

EXHIBIT 7.6 A AND B

Sample Bar Charts

A. Horizontal Bar Chart

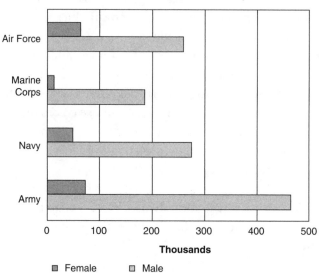

Source: *Statistical Abstract of the U.S.—2010*

B. Vertical Bar Chart

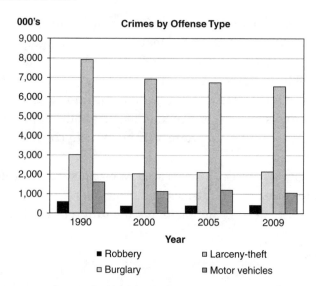

Source: *Statistical Abstract of the U.S.—2010*

EXHIBIT 7.7 A–C

Sample Circle Graphs

A. Shows Proportion of Each Group to Whole

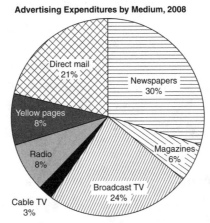

Advertising Expenditures by Medium, 2008

Direct mail 21%
Newspapers 30%
Yellow pages 8%
Magazines 6%
Radio 8%
Broadcast TV 24%
Cable TV 3%

Source: *Statistical Abstract of the U.S.— 2010*

B. Shows Two Separate Groups of Data

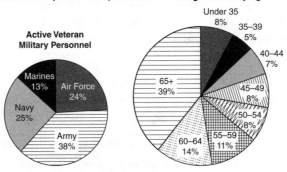

Living Veterans by Age

Active Veteran Military Personnel

Marines 13%
Air Force 24%
Navy 25%
Army 38%

Under 35 8%
35–39 5%
40–44 7%
45–49 8%
50–54 8%
55–59 11%
60–64 14%
65+ 39%

Source: U.S. Department of Defense, 2009

C. Shows Progressive Changes

Coal Consumption by World Area

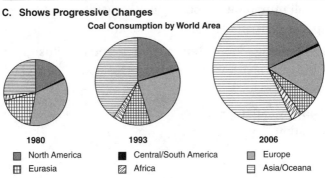

1980   1993   2006

- North America
- Central/South America
- Europe
- Eurasia
- Africa
- Asia/Oceana

Source: World Resources Institute, 2008

Line Graphs—Showing Trends over Time

Line graphs allow readers to see trends in data over time. Although computer programs can construct line graphs, keep these principles in mind:

- Keep the number of lines in the graph to five or fewer.
- Label all lines clearly. Use different patterns or colors that easily distinguish one line from another.
- Label the horizontal axis and vertical axis clearly.

Pictorial or Symbol Graphics—Showing Data in Visual Form

Some of the more common pictorial or symbol graphics include organization and flow charts, maps, photographs, diagrams, and paintings. Organization charts and flow charts are commonly used in business publications, including proposals. In preparing these graphics, follow the guidelines below:

- The symbols should be easy to identify. If you are using the symbol of a machine to represent equipment sales figures, for example, be sure the machine is easy to recognize.
- The symbols should accurately represent differences in size or percentages: their size should be in direct proportion to the amounts they are supposed to represent.
- Label all important elements on an organization or flow chart, map, diagram, photograph, and so on.
- Avoid packing too much information into the illustration. Simplify the chart or picture as much as possible and use the text to elaborate.
- Put any explanations or source notes at the bottom of the illustration.

EXHIBIT 7.8 A–C

Sample Line Graphs

A.

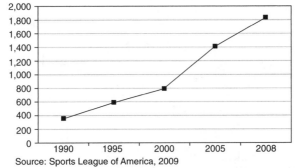

Avg. $ in 000's   Average Professional Football Players' Salaries 1990–2008

Source: Sports League of America, 2009

B.

Mil.$'s   U.S. Consumer Electronic Sales by Product

Source: *Statistical Abstract of the U.S.—2010*

C.

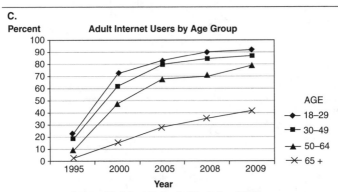

Percent   Adult Internet Users by Age Group

Year

Source: *Statistical Abstract of the U.S.— 2010*

EXHIBIT 7.9 A–C

Sample Pictorial Graphics

A. Sample Organization Chart

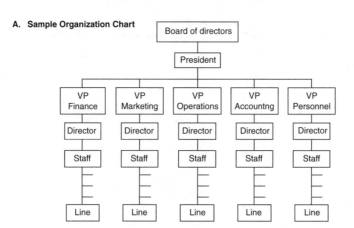

B. Process Flow Chart

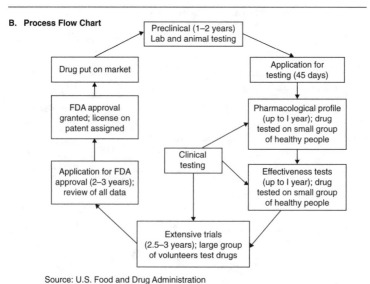

Source: U.S. Food and Drug Administration

C. Sample Image or Icon Chart   **Number of PCs Purchased by Consumers 1995–2009**

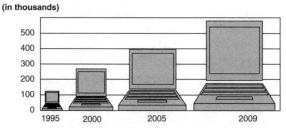

Source: *Statistical Abstract of the U.S.—2010*

FINAL CHECKLIST

No matter how rushed the production schedule, make sure you build in time to check through the proposal carefully before you submit it to the client. Use this checklist to guard against errors.

❑   Has the document been proofread carefully one final time? If possible, have someone proof it who has not seen the document up to this point. Sometimes a new eye catches obvious mistakes everyone else has missed. In one instance, a proofreader noticed that the client's name had been misspelled on the title page. No one else had caught the error through three rounds of review.

❑   Has the numbering of pages and the sequencing of tables and figures been double-checked? Make sure that the page numbers cited in the table of contents are accurate.

❑   Have the latest updated versions of tables, graphics, and appendix material been included? When proposals go through several revisions, it is easy for the wrong versions of a graphic to turn up in the document.

❑   Are there any missing pages? Are any graphics or tables turned the wrong way? Are any appendixes listed but not included?

❑   Is the printing of acceptable quality? Check for blurred print, fuzzy images, or other printing irregularities.

❑   Will the binding hold the document securely?

Now that your proposal has passed this final review, your next step is to present the proposal to the client. Chapter 8 discusses ways to develop and deliver a winning presentation.

8

Making Client Presentations

Laura Chiang stopped by James Mullen's desk.

"Everett Hospital wants us to do a presentation next Tuesday. Ms. Herras just got word from the Director at Everett."

James turned noticeably paler. "Will we have to give part of the presentation?"

"Right before the technical team. Apparently Everett was impressed by our suggested partnership with World Medical Interpreters. They want to hear more."

"But ... I'm lousy at speaking in front of people," James said.

"Don't worry. You should see the schedule Ms. Herras has drawn up for developing the presentation. We'll have so many practice sessions that we'll be able to do this talk backwards."

James looked more hopeful. "I have to admit. We've got a great program for them."

"Then it's time to tell Everett about it."

* * *

Step 9: Presenting the Proposal to the Client

In some instances, you will be asked to make a presentation of your proposal to the client. Whether you realize it or not, a client presentation is actually a sales talk. You are selling the client on three major points:

1. You have a thorough understanding of the client's situation.
2. You have the best solution and benefits to meet the client's needs.
3. Your firm is the best one to do the job.

The client must be convinced that all three points are true. Otherwise, another company is likely to get the project.

Good presentations are a matter of planning, organization, and practice, combined with that elusive quality known as presence, luck, right timing, chemistry, or whatever else it may be called. It is that special rapport you bring to the presentation that tells the client you have absolute confidence in your solution and in your company.

In this chapter we give you guidelines on how to prepare and deliver your presentation. We also include tips on how to prepare for success and how to handle troublesome questions from the client audience.

Planning Steps

Good planning is a critical element of success in any presentation you give. In general, you will need to prepare for the following:

- *The presentation,* given by one or more of your staff members, that outlines the main points of the proposal. This includes preparing any graphics or visuals (transparencies, charts, handouts, and other aids) to illustrate and clarify your main points. The client audience may or may not ask questions during this time.
- A *question-and-answer time* during which the client will quiz you about the proposal's features and your company's capabilities.
- A *wrap-up time* in which you will review the main selling points and try to convince the client that your firm should be selected for the project.

The planning stage begins by answering four basic questions: why are you giving this presentation, to whom are you giving it, what do you plan to say, and where and when will you give the presentation?

Why Are You Giving the Presentation?

At first, the answer seems obvious: The client requested it, and you want to win the bid. But it's worth your while to look deeper and to establish an *objective* for your talk. Every effective presentation is founded on a clear objective.

A presentation can do one or all of the following:

- Educate or inform
- Propose recommendations and gain acceptance
- Initiate action
- Evoke interest
- Interpret, clarify, and evaluate
- Introduce new ideas
- Sell or persuade

These objectives are rather general, and you probably want to achieve a combination of them. But what specifically are you seeking to accomplish in the relatively short time you will have with the client? Take time to put your objectives in writing. A written objective can provide a unifying theme for your entire presentation. Use "to" phrases to state your objectives: to convince, to persuade, to demonstrate, to inform. For example, the objectives below give the presentation team a clear idea of their goals:

- To convince Everett Hospital that our company offers a superior interpreter call network and an effective partnership with an interpreter service to help Everett provide high-quality health care to *all* of its patients.
- To prove to FairValue Hardware that by improving customer service—as well as upgrading major stores—the company can regain its market share and overcome strong competition from rival chains.
- To demonstrate to South Holland Community Hospital that our company's outreach program will attract key patient groups, improve the hospital's financial standing, and create an ongoing need for the hospital's services in the surrounding community above and beyond immediate care facilities.

Writing a good objective is not easy. You can start with an "elevator moment"—what would you say to someone if you had only one minute or less to explain your proposal? Or, at the end of your presentation, what key information do you want the client to remember? What impression do you want to create about your solution and your company? What decisions do you want the client to make?

As you write your objective, keep three criteria in mind: Your objective must be *attainable, measurable,* and *realistic.* Don't try to accomplish too many objectives in one talk. Remember, the more objectives you have, the more tasks are required to accomplish them.

Keep the objective simple. The results of your presentation should be measurable. In the case of a proposal presentation, the measurement yardstick is straightforward: the client accepted your solution and hired your company.

Who Is Your Client Audience?

You began the proposal-writing process by looking at the situation from the client's point of view. This orientation is even more important when it comes to presenting your ideas in person. To do the most effective job, you must know your audience. In general, companies are interested in five main areas:

- Reducing costs
- Increasing return on investment
- Improving quality and performance
- Raising productivity
- Saving time

If you can identify which of these are of *primary* concern to the client, you will begin to mesh your objective with the needs of your audience. Everett Hospital, for instance, may be interested primarily in improving quality and performance, reducing costs, and saving time. The objective of providing Everett with an interpreter call network and a partnership with an outside interpreter service speaks to all three of these needs.

In addition, your background research on the client, and all client contacts that the proposal manager and team have had, will be invaluable when you start preparing for the presentation. This information will tell you who in the client organization is likely to be resistant to your ideas, who may be supportive, and who the major decision makers are.

Go over your checklists and background notes to determine what appears to motivate the client management. What is the tone and philosophy of the organization's culture? Does the client see itself as an innovator, conservative, socially minded, or strictly business-oriented?

The answers to these and other questions will help you to determine how to tailor your presentation to match the characteristics and communication style of your client. For example, if the client president is detail-oriented and you spend all your time on the big picture, the client is likely to perceive you as too vague or as promising too much without explaining how it will all happen.

This planning step is more important than you may think. Many outstanding proposal ideas die on the presentation floor simply because the proposal team forgot to tailor their talk to the client's needs. The proposal manager and the company's liaison to the client must work closely together to develop an effective way to communicate the proposal to the client.

What Do You Plan to Say?

By this time you have established your objective and know a great deal about your intended audience. Having put the proposal together, you also know your topic. At this point, you can ask yourself a few questions to help focus your thinking:

- What does the client already know about this topic?
- What more does the client want to know about it?
- What does the client *need* to know?
- What *doesn't* the client need to know?
- What topics or areas should we avoid?

This is the point at which you should separate what the client *needs* to know from what is simply *nice* to know. For example, Everett Hospital administrators need to know the main features of the health-care interpreter network, but do they need to know how the technical team will solve each problem? Probably not. Only Everett's IT staff are likely to be interested in such details.

The last two points—what the client doesn't need to know and what areas you should avoid—refer to sensitive issues. These are areas that you generally don't want to bring up in the presentation but are prepared to handle should the question-and-answer session reveal them. For instance, if the Everett call manager network is going to tread on another department's territory, the proposal team members may not want to discuss this issue at the presentation. If the client brings it up, however, the proposal team can simply say that they are working on several options to address the problem.

When and Where Is Your Presentation?

For planning purposes, you need to have a firm idea of when and where the presentation is to be given. You then know how much lead time you have to develop the talk. If possible, make up a floor plan of the room where the presentation will be held. This will help you plan where to place your visual aids and what seating arrangements you may encounter. In many instances, however, you may not know exactly where you will be speaking until the day of the presentation.

By knowing the location in advance, you can estimate how much travel time you will need to allow for yourselves and your materials. You should consider one or two alternate routes or forms of transportation that can be used should the unexpected happen. One group of consultants, for example, found their route to the client's office blocked by fire trucks. Luckily, they were able to use their GPS to come up with another route and make the meeting with only a few minutes' delay.

Organizing the Presentation

Once the initial planning steps are complete, you can begin organizing your presentation. You will need to organize the text of your talk and the visual aids you are going to use. In some cases, your presentation may also involve a live demonstration or the use of interactive media. Regardless of the simplicity or sophistication of your proposal topic, however, there are a few basic principles that will help you organize your materials and your team to make an effective proposal presentation.

Organizing the Topic

You have already organized your topic for the written proposal. But an oral presentation involves more than simply reading what you wrote. You need to use an organizational approach tailored to capture an audience's interest and hold their attention throughout the talk. Here are some well-known organizational techniques that should fit your situation:

- *Problem-solution approach*: Start with the current situation (what your client's problems or needs are), move to your solution, and finish with a picture of how the client will benefit by adopting your solution.

- *Descriptive approach:* Begin by describing your solution to the client's problem or need, and then explain what your solution will accomplish, and how it will do so.
- *Best alternative approach:* Describe the client's problem or need, offer several possible alternatives, and then explain why the alternative you chose is the best one for the client's situation.
- *Events approach:* Explain what led up to the client's problem or need, why it happened, and how you will help the client resolve it.
- *Technical approach:* Discuss the client's problem, your approach to the problem, the benefits the client can expect by adopting your approach, and your conclusions and recommendations.

Once you decide on an approach, you can create a rough draft of your presentation either in list form, as an outline, as a computer presentation, on a digital whiteboard, or on other audiovisual media. This will highlight your main points and help you distinguish between what the client *needs* to know versus what is merely *nice* for them to know.

The goal at this stage is to divide your talk into several subtopics. For example, the Integrated Medical Systems team might divide its Everett Hospital presentation into the following topic areas:

1. Everett's needs and vision for a rapid-response interpreter call service to solve the health-care and staff use problems they have identified
2. Current state-of-the-art call management networks and security software, and their limitations
3. Integrated Medical Systems' study of the technical problems and its experience and successes with similar call networks and security software
4. The call networks that IMS has developed and the networks' features, advantages, and results
5. A partnership strategy in which Everett can take advantage of a multilanguage interpreter service via the new call network
6. A wrap-up listing recommendations and results that Everett can achieve with the new network and partnership

By dividing the topic into categories, you can develop a concise, informative outline that addresses all the main points without bogging you down in excessive detail. At this stage, you may want to assign a rough time limit to each topic. In the case above, topics one through three may take only about one-quarter of the time, topics four and five about one-half, and the final wrap-up only about one-quarter. The question-and-answer session would follow.

To keep yourself focused on your objective and outline, ask yourself at each stage of developing your talk, "What does the client absolutely *have* to know about this area? What is important to the client? What can we let go?" This entire process is a series of choices made within the context of limited time and the need to hold client interest.

Creating Text and Visual Aids

Once you have established your main points and developed your text, you must think about the best combination of text and visual aids to convey your presentation. The form of the talk that you take to the presentation will depend a great deal on the individual situation. In some cases, you may be able to use index cards with key facts written on each card. In other cases, overhead transparencies, slides, and a script may be all you will need. In still other instances, the talk may be divided among several people, each one of whom will have his or her own notes, slides, or outlines.

Note cards or notepad notes have the advantage of being easy to delete or amend on the spot. They are relatively unobtrusive and can be slipped in a pocket or briefcase. You can key them to overhead transparencies, slides, computer presentations, or digital whiteboards and use them to jog your memory should you be distracted or forget to cover an essential fact.

Visuals are essential to any presentation. A study conducted by the Wharton School of Business at the University of Pennsylvania proved that presenters using visuals were judged by their audiences to be more professional, persuasive, and credible. Exhibit 8.1 summarizes the advantages and disadvantages of using various types of audiovisual aids in your presentations.

The key element to keep in mind is that visual aids should supplement or enhance your presentation, not serve as the main focus or substitute for content that should be communicated

EXHIBIT 8.1

Advantages/Disadvantages of Audiovisual Aids

Visual Aid	Advantages	Disadvantages
Whiteboards and flip charts	Easy to obtain and use; little or no cost; good audience interaction	Dull; low visibility; limits audience size; low visual impact; wear and tear with use
Digital whiteboards	Very flexible; interactive; multimedia possibilities	Expensive to produce; not portable; high tech
Overhead projectors	Quick and economical; easy to carry and store; projectors available for any size audience; easy to alter or redo	Mechanics of switching visuals can be distracting; projectors can block audience view
Computer presentations	Can be shown in any size meeting; flexible; multimedia possibilities; changes easy to make; cost effective	More add-ons, more can go wrong; power supply and programs can be interrupted; can bore audiences
Video/digital film	Both have high visual impact and high interest level; suit any size audience; multimedia possibilities	Audience focuses on visuals instead of speaker; can be expensive to produce; may require special playback equipment, particularly in foreign countries
Slides	Higher quality than overheads; projectors easy to carry and use; high visual impact; long life; low tech	Darkened room required decreases contact with audience; slides cannot be redone easily; equipment is often noisy
Models, mock-up, props	High impact value; add reality to presentation	Can be costly and time-consuming to prepare; may limit size of audience
Video teleconferencing	Connects two or more locations; saves time and money; enables quicker decisions	Requires high-tech power supply and equipment; may be subject to interruptions or faulty transmission

verbally. Nor should you overwhelm the audience with so many visuals that your main points are lost in a blizzard of color, design, and show-stopping special effects. Use the visual aids for maximum impact, keeping the style and character of your audience in mind.

Organizing Your Team

All team members should know exactly what they are supposed to do for the presentation and when and how they are supposed to do it. This task can be accomplished by creating a matrix that shows which topics are assigned to which team members. If during the development process one team member feels more comfortable with another topic, you can make adjustments. Be sure to have backup team members available among your staff should any team member be unable to perform his or her part of the presentation because of illness, accident, or family emergencies.

It's also a good idea to make each team member responsible for handling client questions about his or her particular area. In this manner, you can direct the client's questions to the person on your team who is the most qualified to answer them. This also frees the other team members to concentrate on their area of expertise and gives the client the impression that you are conducting an effective, well-coordinated company effort.

Taking Care of the Details

Part of organizing your presentation involves such details as remembering extension and power cords, extra markers, extra projector bulbs, scissors, tape, and the countless other supplies you need to support your talk. Draw up a list of the items you must have and put one or two team members in charge of making sure these items are brought to the presentation. *Do not assume that the client will be able to supply what you need.* In fact, if you have to ask, it may damage the professional image you wish to convey. Pay attention to the details.

Practicing the Presentation

Before you go in front of the client, you will need to practice your presentation until you have it down cold. This usually involves at least the following:

- Practicing to refine each talk given by team members
- Role-playing with a critical audience
- Conducting dress rehearsals
- Learning how to relax

Practicing Individual Talks

Note cards, outlines, and visual aids are one thing. Standing up in front of an audience and actually giving the talk is quite another. You need to move smoothly from one point to the next, while coordinating visual aids with your talk—bringing them in at just the right time and changing them when you want to emphasize a point.

All team members should practice their individual talks with other team members to refine the content and to coordinate visual aids. You may find that the talk needs more illustration or less. If someone else is going to work the transparencies, the computer, or the projector or turn the flip charts for you as you speak, how will it be done? Where will the screen and equipment be? How will you signal one another when the right moment occurs?

These details must be worked out well before the talk is given. Once you have a system established, you can adjust it to meet changing conditions. Expecting your partner to guess when and where to change a visual aid is inviting disaster.

Role Playing with a Live Audience

Once the individual talks have been refined by the team, the entire presentation should be given in front of an in-house management audience. The audience's role is to critique the presentation and provide realistic feedback for the team. If you know you will have a problem with one area of your presentation, the audience can act as the client and grill the team on that area until you are satisfied that you can handle any client objections.

It may be grueling to endure such a critiquing session, but it is far better for your own management to find the flaws in your presentation than for the client to do so. Go into these sessions with the idea that you are developing a draft of your talk. The whole purpose of rough drafts is to rip them apart to find the flaws and to make the presentation stronger. The more you can detach your ego from your work, the better your work is likely to become.

Conducting Dress Rehearsals

The final practice stage involves putting all the talks and visual aids together in a setting that resembles the actual client meeting room as closely as possible. This enables you to develop the best arrangement for seating, equipment, and speaker position. Exhibit 8.2 shows examples of meeting room arrangements you may encounter. Notice that the illustrations in the figure show you how to set up your visual equipment so that all members of the audience can easily see the screen, board, or charts. Remember to give careful thought to such matters as glare from windows, the location of electrical outlets, outside noises that might intrude, and so on.

The easier you make it for members of the client audience to see and hear you without distraction, the more of their attention you'll have.

Learning How to Relax

Most people faced with the prospect of speaking in front of others experience a pounding heart, sweaty palms, and nervous tics. In a proposal presentation, you have the added pressure of knowing that an entire job may hang on the outcome of your performance. It's enough to arouse stark terror even in seasoned presenters.

However, there is a secret to managing your fear of public speaking. Notice we said *manage*, not *eliminate*. It's not possible to eliminate all the fear you may feel. But you can learn to manage your emotions enough to find yourself more relaxed and confident in front of the client.

The secret is this: *It is impossible to be physically relaxed and emotionally terrified at the same time.* By relaxing yourself physically, you will automatically relax emotionally.

Follow these three guidelines:

1. *Breathe:* When people are frightened, their breathing becomes shallow and rapid. This reduces oxygen to the brain and interferes with memory and logical thinking. When you change

EXHIBIT 8.2

Typical Seating Arrangements

A. Square Arrangement

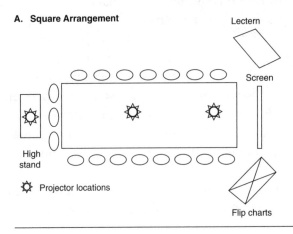

Traditional arrangement with projectors on the table or behind the table, and speakers to one side to allow the audience to view the screen.

High stand

☼ Projector locations

B. U- Shaped Arrangement

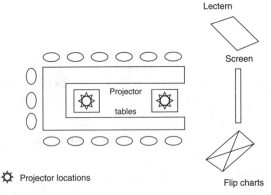

U-shaped arrangement allows projectors to be placed in the center— speaker and screen are clearly visible to everyone in the audience.

☼ Projector locations

C. U- Shaped Arrangement

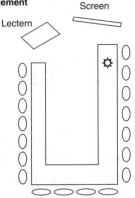

In this arrangement, the projector is placed to one side, forcing the speaker to turn the screen. Audience members on the far side may see a slightly distorted image.

☼ Projector location

your breathing and take slower, deeper breaths, you send more oxygen to your brain and signal your nervous system that the situation is not life-threatening. Your body begins to relax.

2. *Move:* Physical activity burns up the stress hormones released by strong fear. Before the talk, move around, take a brief walk, and stretch your muscles. If you are seated, tense and relax your muscles. Check to see whether you are tensing your neck and shoulders, your jaw, your stomach muscles—if you are, relax them.

3. *Get support:* Agree beforehand to support each other in the presentation. Use inspirational phrases, self-talk, or whatever provides emotional support to you in moments of stress. In the talk, when you feel yourself becoming too anxious, look at the designated friendly face. Emotional support is physically reassuring and will help your body relax.

Keep these three steps in mind throughout the practice sessions so they will be part of your prepresentation warm-up. Write "breathe," "move," and "get support" on your index cards or script so that you will have a visual cue during your part of the presentation.

Remember, when your physical body relaxes, the rest of you relaxes.

Survival Tips

Give yourself an added edge in the presentation by taking a few extra precautions. You want to set up the room so that you know everything is in order for the talk. You also want to be prepared to handle resistance or even hostile reactions the client may throw your way.

If, despite your best efforts, things still go wrong (the computer presentation won't advance, your partner puts up the wrong graphic, a flip chart falls to the floor), stay calm. The more you take such minor disasters in stride, the more your audience will as well. Have a contingency plan in mind should things go wrong.

CHECKLIST: SETTING UP FOR SUCCESS ✓

Here is a quick checklist of steps to take when you arrive at the client's place of business:

❑ Arrange to get into the meeting room early. Plan to arrive half an hour before the talk. This gives you time to adjust to any unexpected situations you may find when you arrive (e.g., a blind corner in the room, construction noise outside, etc.).

❑ Check the physical surroundings of the room. Can you change the order of seats around the tables, rearrange the tables themselves, close the curtains or blinds, or do other tasks to arrange the room for the best presentation?

❑ If the client is to supply you with any equipment—video screens, projectors, teleconferencing equipment, and the like—is it in the room and does it work?

❑ Check all equipment to be sure it works properly. Project an image on a screen or whiteboard to be sure it can be seen from all areas of the room where the client personnel will be sitting. Check the sound level of microphones or multimedia materials.

❑ Check your proposal materials to make sure that they are in the right order, that nothing has been damaged in transit, and that everything is right-side up.

❑ Avoid eating a big meal or drinking cold liquids before your talk. Both items tend to affect the throat and interfere with proper speaking.

❑ Go over the schedule of your presentation one last time with all team members.

Above all, don't call attention to the mistake by blowing up at your partner, obsessing on the missing graphic or transparency, or making too much of the error. *Move on.* Chances are your audience won't think twice about it if you simply go on to the next point. They may even admire your grace under pressure.

Handling Troublesome Questions

What happens when your worst fears are confirmed and the person you thought would cause a problem actually does? Trouble can come in many forms—from mildly voiced objections to outright hostility from someone in the audience. Here are a few suggestions to help you turn the situation to your advantage.

First and foremost, *remain calm.* If your questioner can provoke you, he or she has won the round whether you offer a rebuttal or not. Buy yourself a little time if you need to calm down. Take a drink of water, walk to the other side of the speaker's area, or adjust the microphone. Remember to focus on the issue, not the person who raised it.

Receive all questions cordially. Statements such as, "That's a good question ..." or, "That's a common concern ..." help defuse the situation and put it on more neutral footing.

Listen carefully to the question. Have you really heard what the person is saying or are you distracted by who is saying it or by how it is being said? Listen to the words and the underlying intention. Ask for clarification if you are not sure you understand the issue being raised.

Avoid flip or off-the-cuff answers. Again, buying yourself a little time—a few seconds may be all you need—will give you a chance to ask yourself:

- Why is this question being asked? *Perhaps you were not clear about the point.*
- How does it fit into the objectives of our presentation? *Does the question give you an opportunity to promote your main points again?*
- Can I give a concise, clear answer? *Is there an efficient way to answer the question without appearing curt or flippant?*

Avoid trying to impress or please your audience with a fast rejoinder. A little thought can turn the situation to your favor.

If you don't know an answer, say so—or refer the question to a team member who does know. "That's an excellent point. Brad Shaw is our expert in that area. Brad, what would you say?"

Keep statements "I" centered instead of "you" centered—avoid saying, "You didn't understand that point." Instead, say something like, "I'm glad you asked that question," or, "That's something we considered and had to reject. Let me clarify."

If a questioner appears to be openly hostile or aggressive toward you or any member of your team, stay focused on the issues. You may be asked loaded questions, hypothetical questions, leading questions, or questions designed to derail your presentation. Here's what the experts suggest:

- Use a bridging technique. Move from the hot issue to one you want to talk about. Good bridging statements include:
  "Quite the contrary. Let me show you how we ..."
  "I understand that position, however, ..."
  "We may disagree on that, but a more important point is ..."
- Follow with positive points you want to emphasize that focus on your objective for making the presentation.
- Question the questioner. Sometimes this tactic will reveal the questioner's real motivation. Maybe he or she feels threatened by the changes you are proposing. Find out more about why that person is asking hostile questions.
- If appropriate, use humor to defuse the situation. In some cases, hostile questions can be the result of circumstances— the room is too hot, the session has been a long one, the material may be difficult to follow. A humorous remark that captures a shared sense of frustration can be enough to lighten the atmosphere and bring the audience back to the main focus. However, be very careful with this technique. You must know your audience and feel confident that the humor won't backfire on you. *Never* make a questioner the butt of the joke.
- Stay in control of the exchange. Where you can agree with the questioner, do so, but bring the focus back to the points you want to make. You want to leave the audience with a strong, positive presentation.

CHECKLIST FOR CLIENT PRESENTATIONS ✓

Prior to your presentation, make a quick list of major points to remember. You might draw up a checklist like the following:

☐ Have you established a clear objective for making the presentation?
☐ Do you know the client audience and what you need to say to them?
☐ Have the time and place for the presentation been confirmed?
☐ Have you organized the topic into subtopics?
☐ Have you outlined the talk on cards, on a notepad, or in a script?
☐ Have you selected the best visuals?
☐ Does everyone on the team understand what they are to do?
☐ Have you listed the details you need to remember?
☐ Has the team practiced the talk and conducted a dress rehearsal?
☐ Can you arrive early at the client site to arrange the room and check the equipment?
☐ Have you strategized how to handle troublesome questions?

This final stage in the 9-step process can be just the beginning for you and your firm. This book has offered you an efficient, effective method to help you evaluate RFPs quickly and to find the best jobs that match your firm's marketing strategy and capabilities. You can establish a sound proposal-writing process in your company to help you highlight your solutions and qualifications in a way that catches the client's attention. We hope the guidelines, suggestions, and recommendations in the book will assist you in offering your clients the best services possible.

Today, with more people forming their own businesses and corporations operating on thinner margins, competition for clients is intense. It's up to every entrepreneur and every corporate manager to find opportunities and to create prospects where they may not have existed before. We hope this book helps you along the way.

As the old saying goes: luck favors the prepared!

Appendix A
Sample Executive Summary

The executive summary in this appendix is from a medium-sized consulting firm that specializes in helping firms relocate and design their data processing facilities. Appendix B contains the proposal for this project, and Appendix C shows the résumé boilerplates included with the proposal.

In the executive summary, the proposal team emphasizes the client's needs and the solution that Western Consulting Associates has developed. The company focuses on the complete program of services they provide and their accomplishments in this field. The client not only has a good overview of what the proposal contains but also a strong impression of the company.

Executive Summary

Introduction

Western Consulting Associates proposes a complete program of services to assist Armstrong & Hou Financial, Inc., in the relocation, design, and construction of a new data processing center. We offer a unique set of services that covers the logistics of moving a data processing company; working with architects, engineers, and outside contractors to customize the new facility; and installing and upgrading all computer networks, operating systems, and Web sites. The program will be accomplished in three phases and will produce deliverable results that meet or exceed all technical requirements set forth in the request for proposal. We understand that Armstrong & Hou is working within a very tight schedule to complete the work, and we feel confident that our company can meet the three-month time frame stated in the proposal.

Our three-phase program focuses on the preparation of block diagrams and requirements, detailed requirements for bid specifications, and support for Armstrong & Hou's design and construction bidding process. In addition to providing assistance with the new facility, we also offer Armstrong & Hou continuous support to maintain its data-processing services throughout the relocation and design stages. Western Consulting Associates specializes in maintaining uninterrupted computer services while developing new systems at a relocation site.

Our Approach

The three-phase program that we propose will enable Armstrong & Hou to select the best design for their data center, develop precise specifications for soliciting construction bids, and ensure the most efficient use of the 10,000- to 12,000-square-foot office space purchased in the Chicago area. The data-processing center will be able to provide fully integrated services to all their clients with increased speed and efficiency.

Phase I consists of a close examination of the space requirements to develop the base building and data center designs. This phase also includes establishing criteria for the selection of environmental support equipment and completing specific documents for all facets of construction (e.g., electrical, plumbing, fire protection, and security interfaces).

Phase II involves creating detailed requirements from which Armstrong & Hou's architect and engineer can develop a bid specifications package. Our consultants have devised a particularly time-saving method of determining how to select bids from among those solicited.

Phase III, which will be initiated once Phases I and II have been approved by Armstrong & Hou, consists of support for the firm's design and construction process. We will help Armstrong & Hou's staff review bid specifications for conformance to project requirements and adjust the design to the firm's configuration.

To accomplish the tasks in Phases I and II, we will form a joint Western-Armstrong & Hou task force that will report directly to the president of Armstrong & Hou. We will hold weekly review meetings with the firm's staff and work closely with their technical group. Such coordination will enable us to stay on schedule and solve in a timely manner any problems that arise.

Proposed Project Results

Once Phases I and II have been completed, we will present Armstrong & Hou with a set of design drawings and requirement books. These include:

- *Phase I:* Block diagrams of computer room, total loads for computer room, requirements for closets; design development documents and blueprints for electrical supply, security, fire protection, and high-voltage AC.
- *Phase II:* One-quarter-inch layout and recommended considerations for computer room and adjacent area; list of workstation components; requirements for the raised floor, hung ceiling, and electrical layout; and plans for security, fire protection, high-voltage AC, specialty plumbing, and vendor selection.

Management Section

To ensure that the project proceeds smoothly, we will form a task force with Armstrong & Hou's senior management to maintain close communication throughout the three phases of the work. We will appoint a project manager to oversee all aspects of the relocation from design to installation. The manager will be on-site at all times to make sure that assigned tasks are completed, all time schedules are met, and all phases of the project are completed to the client's complete satisfaction.

Time and Cost Overview

We anticipate meeting Armstrong & Hou's schedule of complet-ing Phases I and II by October 15 and Phase III five weeks later after receiving approval to proceed with the final stage. Our exten-sive experience with relocation and design projects often enables us to streamline work tasks without compromising safety and quality.

Our pricing structure is based on standard industry practices of quoting a fee for each phase of the project. Our fees include sup-port for all design work, bid specifications, and vendor selection until the design center is completed. All out-of-pocket expenses incurred by Western Consulting Associates on behalf of Armstrong & Hou will be billed at actual cost. The proposal pricing, configura-tion, and terms stated are valid for 60 days from the date on the cover of the proposal.

Western Consulting Associates

Western Consulting Associates was founded in 1970 to assist firms in the process of relocating and designing their computer and data processing facilities. Today, our firm is recognized internationally as one of the leading companies in this field. We have pioneered many of the current techniques used to design data center layouts, safeguard power systems, and provide security systems that prevent the loss of key data during transfer. We have experience with a wide range of mainframes, servers, and interactive networks used by firms similar to Armstrong & Hou.

The relocation and design of a data-processing facility is a highly complex and specialized task that requires an experienced, dedicated team and close coordination between the company staff and consultants. We believe that Western Consulting Associates offers a unique blend of experience, expertise, and custom services to meet Armstrong & Hou's requirements for this project.

Appendix B
Sample Proposal

The proposal in this appendix is from a medium-sized consulting firm that specializes in the relocation and design of data-processing facilities. The client has requested a proposal for moving their facilities from one city to another. Appendix A contains the executive summary for this proposal; Appendix C contains résumé boilerplates that would be included in the proposal document.

Because the project focuses primarily on steps involved in relocating and designing a data-processing facility, the proposal writers use an outline form. This approach makes it easy for the client to see the major steps involved in each phase and what to expect in terms of tasks, costs, and results.

For this type of project, the technical section consists of the work plan, while the management section outlines the tasks required to complete the first two phases of work. The time and cost estimates are also brief, usually with a nonitemized budget included to show major cost categories and estimated fees. The client can then request a more detailed breakdown of time, cost, and management issues at a later date.

Response to Requirements
DATA CENTER DESIGN

Armstrong & Hou Financial, Inc.
Armstrong International Building
34 Silver Plaza Drive
Alamagordo, TX 50221

Mr. Calvin T. Schwartz
President

Proposal Submitted
by

Western Consulting Associates
142 Riverside Business Court
Houston, TX 56621
Armstrong & Hou Proposal No: 69–002

May 23, 20—

TABLE OF CONTENTS

Page No.

I. Our Understanding of the Situation

As a result of our examination of the Request for Proposal and our conversations with Armstrong & Hou Financial, Inc., management, we have developed the following understanding of the company's situation:

- Armstrong & Hou Financial, Inc., currently operates a large-scale data center in the Armstrong & Hou International Building, which serves users throughout the country.
- Armstrong & Hou Financial, Inc., plans to relocate this operation to a new facility located in Chicago. This new facility will serve all current user sites.
- The area required for the new center, its environmental support equipment, and the associated administrative space will comprise about 10,000 to 12,000 square feet.
- Armstrong & Hou Financial, Inc., Data Center schedule requires the completion of block diagrams, loads, and directions for base building support services by October 15. Thirty (30) days after that date, the architectural engineering firm of Hanover and Wyle will need detailed specifications to prepare its center designs and bid packages.

Armstrong & Hou Financial, Inc., is seeking assistance from Western Consulting Associates to help its engineers, architects, and vendors expedite the design and construction of the storage, computer support, and machine rooms of this data center. This required assistance does not include the design of offices, communications cubicles, or market data communications rooms outside of the main computer room.

II. Objectives of the Project

The proposed project's major objectives are divided into three phases:

II.1 Phase I

Prepare a set of block diagrams and requirements to be used to develop the base building and data center designs. Specifically:

- Current and future space requirements
- Decision data for Armstrong & Hou Financial, Inc.'s (AHF) use in selecting environmental support equipment
- Data center design development requirements documents, (including architectural and mechanical, electrical, and plumbing approaches; fire protection; and specialized security interface)

II.2 Phase II

Develop detailed requirements from which AHF's architects and engineers can develop a bid specifications package. This includes detailed:

- Architectural requirements
- Mechanical requirements
- Electrical requirements
- Plumbing requirements
- Fire protection requirements
- Security and monitoring requirements

II.3 Phase III

Support AHF's design and construction efforts by:

- Reviewing bid specifications for conformance to project requirements
- Applying enhancements and changes resulting from the AHF computer configuration adjustments

III. Technical Section

III.1 Phases I–III: Work Plan Summaries

Phase I: Data Center Design Development Requirements
Five essential activities are needed to develop the data center requirements and to achieve deliverable results. These activities are:

1. Develop data center space programs based upon current and future space requirements and associated workflows.

2. Review data center hardware and adjunct workstation layouts to address:
   - Projected computer capacity requirements
   - Operational effectiveness
   - Physical security
3. Provide decision data:
   - Identify in business terms the pros and cons associated with specific layouts and environmental systems approaches
   - How to select the design approach
4. Prepare data center design development requirements and block diagrams. Requirements are needed for the following elements:
   - Exterior walls
   - Ramps
   - Ceiling heights
   - Floor loading
   - Uninterrupted power supply
   - Emergency power
   - Routing of mechanical, electrical, and telecommunications equipment

   Block diagrams are needed for:
   - Computer rooms
   - Supporting space
5. Conduct weekly process meetings with AHF and its architects and engineers.

Phase II: Data Center Detailed Requirements

Develop work products required by AHF's architects and engineers for their development of the data center bid package. This will include:

1. Prepare Phase II work products, including detailed
   - Architectural requirements
   - Mechanical requirements
   - Electrical requirements
   - Plumbing requirements
   - Fire protection requirements
   - Security and monitoring requirements

2. Review work products with AHF
3. Present work products to AHF's architects and engineers
4. Phase II: Data center detailed requirements

The activities in this phase will include:

1. Review bid package drawings and applications for conformance to project scope
2. Provide comments and present bid package to AHF's architects and engineers
3. Review proposed AHF modifications to the design requirements resulting from hardware and technology changes and the like, and coordinate changes with the architects and engineers

III.2 Phases I–III: Work Plan Details

Phase I: Data Center Design Development Requirements

1. Gather Planning Information

Define Planned Work Flows
Develop planned work flow through each MIS area:

- Computer room
- Adjacent office area
- Adjacent storage and work areas

Develop Initial Program Estimates

- Review AHF's assumptions used to arrive at the planned space estimates and evaluate facility requirements in light of those assumptions.
- Develop projections of computer facility requirements based upon:
  - Expected effects of changing technology on facility requirements
  - Space required for hardware transitions
- Identify key cabling distance constraints.

Develop Decision Data

- Develop decision data for selecting the methods for providing computer room power protection, mechanical services, security, and fire suppression considering:
  - Power protection alternatives
  - Installation, maintenance, and equipment cost planning estimates for Halon and dry pipe systems
  - Risks
  - Backup site/contingency plan arrangements
  - Cabling and floor loading requirements
  - Availability of separate base building feeds for electrical, mechanical, and telecommunications services

2. Identify Strategic Decision Issues for Layout

On the basis of information obtained, we will identify strategic decisions that Armstrong & Hou Financial, Inc., must make prior to completing the layout and remaining designs. We already anticipate that these decisions will include:

- Level of flexibility to accommodate business and technical changes
- Location of data center
- Level of redundancy
- Level of power protection required (current and future)
- Fire protection

In addition, we expect that other issues may arise from our data-gathering efforts. For each issue we will research and articulate alternatives and their pros and cons for AHF's consideration.

3. Present Alternatives for Decision Making

We will present written and oral materials describing alternatives to facilitate the decision-making process for Armstrong & Hou Financial, Inc.'s management.

4. Armstrong & Hou Financial, Inc., Communicates Its Decisions

Once Armstrong & Hou Financial, Inc.'s management has

communicated its decisions, we will incorporate these decisions into the remaining design requirements.

5. Complete the Phase I Work Products

a. Complete the space requirements.
    - Complete the space planning requirements for the data center to allow the architects and engineers to begin base building drawings.
b. Electrical planning.
    - Complete the electrical design development requirements within the data center. These include:
        ◦ Computer grounding requirements
        ◦ Requirements for emergency power and uninterrupted power supply
c. Complete the remaining work products.
    - Architectural requirements:
        ◦ Raised floor height and loads
        ◦ Exterior partition and wall approaches
    - Security system requirements:
        ◦ Building interconnection approaches for alarms, detection, and recordings
    - Fire protection requirements:
        ◦ Halon/dry pipe approach requirements
    - High-voltage AC and plumbing requirements:
        ◦ Availability requirements
        ◦ Routing of services to computer room

Phase II: Data Center Detailed Requirements

1. Complete the Phase II work products.
    a. Complete space requirements
        - Complete the space planning requirements for the data center to allow the architects and engineers to begin bid package drawings. Completing the workstation requirements for this task would include:
            ◦ Special lighting

- Telephone and intercom
- Console power requirements
- Alarm panel
- Security monitors
- Partitions
- Special doorways
- Complete the 1/4 scale hardware device layout
- Review locations and capacities for data center phone, power, and, if applicable, terminal cable distribution

b. Electrical planning
- Complete the electrical requirements within the data center. This includes:
  - Review of cabling diagrams for the data center
  - Computer grounding requirements
  - Requirements for emergency power-off controls

c. Complete the remaining work products
- Architectural requirements:
  - Raised floor
  - Hung ceiling
- Security system requirements:
  - Alarms, detection, and recordings
  - Special access control
- Fire protection requirements:
  - Interconnecting to other systems
- High-voltage AC and plumbing requirements:
  - Pipe routing
  - Flood protection

d. Vendor selection
- Identify vendors and the pros and cons associated with specialty equipment to be used

2. Review work products with Armstrong & Hou's management group.
3. Present work products to Armstrong & Hou's architects and engineers.

Phase III: Design Monitoring

1. Review bid package drawings and applications with Armstrong & Hou Financial, Inc.'s management group to make sure they conform to project scope.

2. Discuss the results of the review with AHF's architects and engineers.
3. If there are any technology changes, review AHF's proposed modifications to the design requirements.
4. Coordinate these changes with AHF's architects and engineers.

IV. Project Results

Completion of the data center design process in Phases III. 1 and III. 2 above will produce a set of deliverable drawings and requirements. These results include the following:

IV.1 Stage I

1. Block diagrams of computer room
   - Space layouts
   - Equipment distribution
2. Total loads for computer room
   - Kilowatts
   - BTU levels
   - Weight
3. Requirements for closets
   - Location and capacities or circuit closets for:
     - Power
     - Signal
     - Phone/data
4. Design development documents and sketches for:
   - Electrical
     - Uninterrupted power supply
     - Emergency power
   - Security
   - Fire protection
   - High-voltage AC
5. Weekly status meetings with AHF and its architects and engineers to review progress and to refine schedules for completion of work products and support data gathering.

IV.2 Stage II

1. One-quarter-inch layout and recommend considerations for computer room and adjacent area.
2. List of workstation components to be included for each workstation, such as:
   - Consoles
   - Special furniture and fixtures
   - Special lighting requirements
   - Telephone and/or intercoms
   - Alarm panels
   - Security monitors
   - Partitions
   - Special doorways
3. Raised floor requirements:
   - Grid starting point
   - Ramps and stairs (if applicable)
   - Depth, composition, and cell and stringer system requirements
   - Slab sealing and cleaning requirements
4. Hung ceiling requirements:
   - Material requirements
   - Composition and depth requirements for the cavity
   - Grid layout requirements
5. Electrical requirements
   - Load projections for:
     - Computers
     - High-voltage AC
     - Lighting
   - Clean power and special protection requirements including:
     - Power distribution units and circuits
     - Motor generator sets
     - Emergency power-off controls and circuits
     - Special grounding and fault isolation
     - Power protection alternatives:
       - Costs
       - Space, weight, and environmental characteristics

- Historical reliability and availability
- Statistics
- Detailed machine requirements: We will assemble the manufacturer specifications for the equipment models and identify receptacles, and provide tables for designing power distribution unit configurations.

6. Security systems plans including:
   - Requirements for detection, alarms, and recording of environmental system failures and out of tolerance conditions (e.g., air-conditioning unit failures, water leaks, etc.)
   - Requirements for special data center access control

7. Fire protection systems including:
   - Cost/benefit trade-offs for backup fire protection methods (e.g., Halon and dry-pipe systems) to other available systems

8. High-voltage AC system requirements:
   - General high-voltage AC requirements including:
     - Projected capacities for computer room air-conditioning
     - Levels of redundancy in capacity, external dry-coolers, and pumps
     - Piping routing requirements
     - Special requirements for air handler installation (e.g., floor stands, etc.)

9. Specialty plumbing including:
   - Layouts under raised floors
   - Requirements for floor drains

10. Vendor selections
    - Chart of specialized equipment vendors

V. Management Section

Western Consulting Associates (Western) will maintain close contact with senior management at Armstrong & Hou Financial, Inc., to coordinate all phases of the project.

V.1 Phase I

1. Create task force composed of senior Western and Armstrong & Hou personnel to oversee the project work.

2. Western will appoint a project manager who will coordinate activities at both sites and ensure that the work proceeds smoothly. The manager's responsibilities include:

    - Establishing a project schedule and timeline for each task
    - Assigning all tasks to team members
    - Requiring regular reports from team members on progress
    - Coordinating tasks among outside contractors
    - Holding weekly meetings with AHF managers to keep them informed

V.2 Phase II

The project manager's responsibilities for Phase II include the following:

1. Draw up a schedule and timeline for preparing Phase II work products to enable AHF architects and engineers to develop their data center bid package
2. Meet with AHF to review all architectural, mechanical, engineering, plumbing, fire, and security work products
3. Present final work products to AHF architects and engineers
4. Hold weekly meetings with AHF management

V.3 Phase III

The project manager's responsibilities for Phase III include the following:

1. Assign a task group to review the bid package drawings and applications to ensure that they conform to project scope
2. Present comments to AHF's architects and engineers
3. Assign a task group to monitor technology changes to be incorporated into the final bid package
4. Negotiate the bid package with outside contractors
5. Oversee construction work on the data design center

VI. Time and Cost Estimates

The following time and cost estimates are based on the RFP requirements and our experience with similar projects.

VI.1 Time

The proposal team will complete the project in a timely manner, providing Armstrong & Hou Financial, Inc., with design development requirements by October 15 and with the data center detailed requirements within five weeks after receiving instructions from Armstrong & Hou Financial, Inc., to proceed with the work.

VI.2 Costs

Below is a nonitemized budget of our estimated expenses for all phases.

Nonitemized Budget for Data Center Design

Item	Cost	
Personnel	$208,472	
Relocation and All Data Center Plan Development (6% flat fee of total construction cost—see *Note*)	207,025	
Hardware	36,050	
Software	44,665	
Prototype Field Testing: (OS/Web site/relocated equipment/software)	22,830	
Project Management	99,050	
Design and Monitoring	66,650	
General and Administration*	62,426	
Taxes	9,776	
% Overhead Applied	21,250	
Total Direct Cost		$778,194
Total Indirect Cost (18.1%)	$140,853	
TOTAL COST		**$919,047**

* G&A does not include salaries; that is a separate line item.
Note: Total construction cost determined by AHF is $3,450,417.

Within three months following the conclusion of contracted services and the submission of a final billing for these services, a project audit will be performed by Western Consulting Associates.

Any expenses not previously billed will be invoiced to Armstrong & Hou Financial, Inc., at that time.

VII. Organization and Staffing

A key element in our approach to this project is the assignment of senior personnel who have significant data center design, planning, operations, and management experience. We have selected a project team that not only possesses a seasoned, realistic perspective but also can provide practical suggestions for improvement in such areas as workstation layouts, data center construction, and testing. The project team will consist of the following personnel:

Engagement Director	Dr. Ashok Nalamwar, Partner
Facility Requirements	Thomas S. Mitchell, Associate
Hardware and Network	Harold Kim Chee, Managing Partner
Configuration Planning	A. Carla Washington, Senior Consultant

We will report directly to Mr. Calvin T. Schwartz, president of Armstrong & Hou Financial, Inc. Because of the importance of this project for both organizations, Dr. Ashok Nalamwar, a Partner of our firm, has been assigned overall responsibility for this project.

We are anticipating that Armstrong & Hou Financial, Inc., personnel, architects, and engineers will be available to work with us. Such coordinated teamwork will greatly assist our data-gathering efforts during the early weeks of the project.

VIII. Our Experience and Qualifications

We believe that Western Consulting Associates is well qualified for this assignment. We have managed numerous data center design, construction, and relocation projects for organizations similar to Armstrong & Hou Financial, Inc. These firms include:

- Arthur D. Young & Company
- Ceco Corporation
- C. J. Lawrence, Morgan Grenfell, Inc.
- Crown Consolidated Industries

- Dean Witter Reynolds, Inc.
- Dollar Dry Dock
- G. D. Searle
- Glaxo, Inc.
- Memorial Sloan-Kettering Cancer Center
- Ogilvy and Mather
- Shearson Lehman Hutton
- Thomas and Betts
- Thomas McKinnon Securities, Inc.

Appendix A describes some of our most representative client assignments.

In addition, Western Consulting Associates project team members all have strong backgrounds in data processing operations and technical support management. Our senior staff has an average of 20 years experience in all areas of data center relocation, design, operations, systems, applications, technical support, and administration. Appendix B contains the résumés of project team members.

Appendixes

Appendix A: Representative Client Assignments

During the past three years, we have conducted fourteen data center design assignments. The services we provided ranged from assisting our clients and their architectural engineers in formulating the designs through preparation of all construction documents and on-site supervision of construction and facility testing.

Arthur Young & Company
We developed the data center layout and prepared architectural and engineering plans for 8,500 square feet of data center space and 40,000 square feet of adjacent office space to support its national headquarters MIS, accounting offices, and training center.

Memorial Sloan-Kettering Cancer Center

- *Site selection:* We were responsible for the evaluation of several potential data center site locations. Our study addressed availability of transportation services, communications, electrical power quality, availability of personnel, safety, and personnel services.

- *Designs:* We were asked by the hospital's facility management group to prepare the data center facility design requirements for a 17,000-square-foot facility and relocation plan consisting of over 800 specific tasks. The plan addressed the establishment of the new server-based facility located off-campus, reconfiguration of the present facility to support a reduced workload, and the establishment of satellite data centers for remote processing.
- *Architecture and engineering:* We prepared the architectural and engineering drawings for construction activities and monitored facility testing for uninterrupted power supply, Halon, high-voltage AC, and access systems.

Shearson Lehman Hutton

The client was in its third phase of planning for a 1 million-square-foot data center, designed initially to support a configuration consisting of three IBM mainframes. The network was composed of 26 TI and T3 lines and 9,600 twisted copper pairs. Our assignment included:

- Preparing construction bid specifications and a disciplined procedure for the installation and testing of the network control facility
- Assisting the client's staff in translating telecommunications design concepts into specific drawings and equipment specifications

Our role up to the production changes included:
- Monitoring and revising the plan to address external factors (such as strikes and vendor slippages).
- Reviewing key project deliverables.
- Assisting in coordinating user testing and final changes.

We completed a second project for Shearson Lehman to relocate its commercial paper operations from a remote site into the centralized MIS facility mentioned above. The configuration consisted of a dual HP server complex with an international network consisting of 15 lines terminating at 9 locations. Our assignment included:

- Designing a 15,000-square-foot data center layout for hardware and support functions
- Evaluating growth and associated workload and recommending hardware configurations

Thomas McKinnon Securities, Inc.

Thomas McKinnon Securities and its outside architects and engineers asked us to provide detailed requirements for its 22,000-square-foot data center designed for two TI macro stations. The time frame was extremely tight and required the coordination of our deliverables with the client and the architectural and engineering firms. Our work products were used directly by these firms to begin their designs, construction drawings, and equipment orders.

The work products included projections of hardware configurations over a 10-year period, research on cost trade-offs of alternative fire protection and electrical protection systems, detailed requirements for electrical, mechanical, plumbing, security, fire suppression, monitoring, and cabling, along with data used to select equipment vendors.

Once the initial bid package was prepared by the architectural and engineering firm, we conducted a detailed review to determine conformance with the original requirements.

Appendix B: Project Staff Résumés

Note: In your proposal, your project staff résumés will go here. See Appendix C: Sample Résumé Boilerplates for sample staff résumés that would accompany the sample proposal.

Appendix C
Sample Résumé Boilerplates

The following résumés are examples of boilerplate files that are included with a proposal (in the samples, all names are fictitious). The résumés can be tailored to emphasize staff experience in different areas as required by the proposal. Résumés on file are easy to update and can be reformatted for any type of document. (Appendix B contains a sample proposal for these résumés; Appendix A contains the executive summary for the proposal.)

When assembling résumés for your proposal, place them according to rank, usually as follows:

President/partner	Vice president
Associate	Managing partner/director
Staff specialist (e.g., technical expert, physician, outside contractor)	Consultants
Support staff (if required)	

Résumés can vary in length from one page to several pages, depending on the project and on the information the client needs to know about your project staff. You want to show that staff members have the required credentials, experience, and ingenuity to complete the work to the client's satisfaction. Résumé formats can vary but should always be clear and concise.

Armstrong & Hou Financial, Inc.
Data Center Design   Dr. Ashok Nalamwar

DR. ASHOK NALAMWAR

Dr. Nalamwar is a Partner of Western Consulting Associates. He received his BS, MS, and Ph.D. from Stanford University. Dr. Nalamwar has 24 years of data processing experience in the banking, brokerage, insurance, medical, pharmaceutical, and manufacturing industries.

Dr. Nalamwar's experience has been in IBM mainframe and server technical support, hardware and facilities planning, management and technical consulting, computer operations, applications development, distributed processing system support, and micro system support. He also has experience in relocating TI, UNISYS, HP, IBM, Macintosh, and Prime Systems.

MAJOR PROFESSIONAL ACCOMPLISHMENTS

As a management consultant, Dr. Nalamwar has participated in the planning and execution of four recent computer center relocations.

Major International Financial Services Firm
Consolidated data processing facilities from four sites into a single newly constructed facility in London, England. The relocation was an upgrade from multiple dual TIs and the phased cutover of HP and IBM systems. The data center supported online systems for New York, European, and Asian operations. Dr. Nalamwar's responsibilities included:

- Development of project planning charts for each phase of the relocation
- Development of all online, batch, and network testing and verification strategies
- Project management including review of deliverables, task accounts and schedules, and management reporting on progress
- Implementation of a project management system for contract and scheduling of all tasks

Major Pharmaceutical Firm

Relocated the client's computer center and its operations, technical, and network support staff to a newly renovated site within Chicago. The facility supported two IBM mainframes with online users from coast to coast and throughout the country. Extremely tight controls were required as the cutover was conducted on a regular two-day weekend and involved moving many critical devices. Dr. Nalamwar's responsibilities were:

- Expansion of existing task list from approximately 90 to 300 tasks
- Implementation of project management systems for project scheduling control
- Assisted all project team members in defining deliverable requirements and formats
- Coordination of hardware vendor meetings
- Review of all task deliverables, project management system updating and analysis, and project status reporting

Major Manufacturing Firm

The firm's entire computer center, support, and development staff were relocated within Chicago to a newly constructed building and computer facility. A prerequisite to relocation was the need to consolidate from multiple IBM mainframes to a single mainframe. Dr. Nalamwar's responsibilities were:

- Interviewing users and evaluating requirements for a nondisruptive move
- Development of processor replacement and relocation strategies and management support during the decision-making process
- Development of detailed task descriptions and planning charts for the processor swap and data center relocation
- Assisting the client in the implementation and initial execution of a project management system

Major Medical Center

Dr. Nalamwar assisted in decentralizing the medical center's data-processing center. The existing mainframe now runs at the New York site, and a TI server system has been installed in a new facility in New Jersey. He developed plans to upgrade later to an enhanced system configuration. All online applications were relocated to the new computer center. Dr. Nalamwar's major responsibilities were:

- Project manager for the relocation assignment tasks, deliverable dates, reviews, plan administration, and status reporting
- Design of computer room hardware layout, workstation layouts, and office and storage layouts
- Implementation of the relocation project management system
- Development of a detailed hour-by-hour migration plan
- Creation of an application migration strategy and test plan
- Establishment of revised operational procedures for the coordination of both data centers

PRIOR EXPERIENCE IN DATA PROCESSING

Prior to joining Western Consulting Associates, Dr. Nalamwar had a distinguished career in data processing. Among his more outstanding technical accomplishments are the following:

Major Commercial Bank
- Developed a quality assurance and control function for a centralized operation of 18 HP and VAX systems that was being expanded to 28 systems. Developed and implemented standards that addressed operating procedures, user applications, and operations interfacing, security, backups and restorers, and management controls.
- As an operating system software project manager, responsible for the development and maintenance of all in-house system software and common subroutines, the analysis and implementation of vendor program products, and the creation of standards and procedures related to their use.
- As manager of facilities and hardware planning, was responsible for:
  - Acquisition of all hardware for both the data center and all user areas. Major upgrades were made to the systems during the migration period.
  - Vendor and trade support of all environmental systems, including a diesel-operated uninterrupted power supply to maintain air-conditioning and fire protection systems.

- As project leader for online trust system supporting 200 terminals, dealt with all maintenance for the database-oriented portion of the system, performance tuning and enhancement to support end-user processing.
- Performed capacity study for the employee benefit and trust accounting and reporting system to determine the impacts and requirements associated with the integration of the personal trust system. The study addressed processor, auxiliary storage, network, response time, and batch throughput capacity issues.

National Facility Management Company

- *Major insurance company*: Responsible for the development of a plan to move all the OS software from New York City to a new data-processing center in Roanoke, Virginia. The task included the testing and verification of all hardware, software, and data following the move. This plan was executed starting with the close of business on a Friday and was operational the following Monday morning in a new facility.
- *Major brokerage firms*: The clients commissioned a joint study to develop and implement a mainframe-to-mainframe inquiry and retrieval facility. This task was part of a data processing start-up project for both clients' sites.
- *Major consumer products manufacturer*: Responsible for the start-up of a facility to support new systems development and production processing. This task involved the implementation of all support facilities, training of operations and application staff, and development of standards and procedures for operating, controlling, and securing the operation. The facility was up and running in two weeks. Two months later, the first new application was in production.

Armstrong & Hou Financial, Inc.
Data Center Design   Thomas S. Mitchell

THOMAS S. MITCHELL

Mr. Mitchell is an Associate of Western Consulting Associates. He holds a BS degree from Carnegie Mellon University of Pittsburgh, and an MS degree from the University of Illinois, Urbana. He has 17 years experience in data processing in the manufacturing, financial services, and telecommunications industries. His areas of expertise include management consulting, data processing operations, hardware planning, and applications development.

MAJOR PROFESSIONAL ACCOMPLISHMENTS

Mr. Mitchell's major consulting achievements include the following:
- Developed Western Consulting Associates' approach to computer center relocation, consolidation, and design.
  In the past five years, he developed relocation plans for:
  - Three major brokerage firms
  - Two major banks
  - Several manufacturers

Major Brokerage Firm
Prepared the consolidation plan for a major brokerage firm which relocated its data center from New York to Dallas, established a large satellite network to a corporate network, and absorbed the data processing for a large credit card and banking subsidiary.

Major Medical Center
Prepared the data center facility design and relocation plans for a large medical center. The plan addressed establishing the new HP-based facility located off-campus, reconfiguring the present on-campus facility to support a reduced workload, and establishing satellite centers for remote processing

Major Commercial Bank
Developed and integrated technical, operational, and facilities plan for the client's multiple data centers to address cost reduction,

security, growth, disaster recovery, and business risk associated with relocation and consolidation. The study led to a multimillion-dollar reduction in operating costs, improved security, additional capacity to meet growth, and an improved image for marketing the bank's services.

Major Domestic Conglomerate

Mr. Mitchell has been retained as an ongoing consultant to assist this $1.2 billion diversified organization in its annual MIS strategic planning process. He and the organization's staff are implementing several key procedures, including:

- Improved payback associated with development projects, and software and hardware upgrades
- Improved responsiveness of MIS to changing business needs
- Improved information and processing security

Cellular Telephone Services Supplier

Reviewed the implementation and production support of the primary business system for this Fortune 10 company. The study led to applications systems revisions, a reorganization of the applications maintenance and operations support functions, relocation of the application to a more stable operating environment, and modifications to user operating procedures. Customer service levels were improved, and key clients were served more efficiently.

Large Investment Bank

Performed a comprehensive security review of the trading, research, office automation, and back office systems to identify physical, data, application, software, and operational exposures. The findings showed major risks of disclosure, operational disruptions, and tampering. A practical approach to address these exposures was developed and implemented.

Major Pharmaceutical Firm

Developed the contingency plan strategy and implementation plan for this large-scale IBM, HP, and Prime-based firm. This involved selection of methods to switch its on-campus IBM Token Ring, Ethernet, and remote network to a backup site; preparation of detailed procedures that have to be in place prior to execution of a disaster recovery; and development of procedures to keep the plan current. The company has recently conducted the first test and is working toward the plan completion.

PRIOR EXPERIENCE IN DATA PROCESSING

Before joining Western Consulting Associates, Mr. Mitchell acquired the following data processing operations experience.

First National Bank

As manager of hardware and capacity planning, he was responsible for capacity hardware planning studies on methods to increase capacity in growth-environment hardware; implementation of storage management operational performance and capacity reporting; and implementation of various software systems.

Inland Steel

As a project leader of system software, he was responsible for implementation and support of an automated data-processing production control system within multiple data centers. Prior to holding this position, he was an operations analyst during the conversion of all corporate systems to IBM processors and an ASP environment. Responsibilities included diagnosis and resolution of hardware, applications, operational, and system software problems. He has also held positions at U.S. Steel as an applications programmer/analyst supporting online order entry and sales analysis systems.

Armstrong & Hou Financial, Inc.
Data Centered Design   Harold Kim Chee

HAROLD KIM CHEE

Mr. Chee is a Managing Partner with the Information Services Group of Western Consulting Associates. He received his BS degree from Ohio University and his MS and MBA degrees from Michigan State University. He has 17 years of experience in data processing.

Mr. Chee's technical experience has been in large-scale mainframe online and network support, telecommunications, server systems, hardware, facilities planning, and applications development. His management work has focused on overseeing distributed processing operations, money transfer wire rooms, check processing, and large-scale data centers.

MAJOR PROFESSIONAL ACCOMPLISHMENTS

Mr. Chee's most recent consulting achievements for data-processing projects include the following.

Major Brokerage Firm
Responsible for the phase-over installation and testing for one of the largest brokerage data centers in New York. As a senior consultant for this effort, Mr. Chee:

- Developed short- and long-term communications equipment requirements and the firm's associated cabling, space, electrical, and mechanical loads (both primary and backup)
- Developed architectural and engineering requirements including:
    - Hardware configuration and layouts for network equipment
    - Workstation components within network control facilities
    - Cabling specifications for office areas, interconnections between communications equipment, voice distribution rooms, and cabling distribution rooms for fiber and copper circuits
    - Fiber/copper facilities within the building riser systems
    - Electrical requirements for power protection, lightning, grounding
    - Vendor selection considerations

- Developed implementation plans to accomplish the network phase-over and coordinated external/in-house network installation, site construction/testing activities, and computer equipment installation/testing
- Site supervision of network construction activities

Major Brokerage Firm, London, England

Consolidated all business functions, technical support, and computer and telecommunications services of this international firm from five locations to a single new facility. This included multiple data centers (IBM, HP) and a global telecommunications network to support the new facility and all European and Far East branches. Mr. Chee's specific responsibilities included:

- Developing detailed plans for installation and testing of the telecommunications hardware for voice/data systems
- Coordinating vendor activities among multiple vendors and suppliers
- Coordinating testing among United States, European, and Far Eastern branches

Major Pharmaceutical Firm

Develop detailed plan to relocate the firm into a 14,500-square-foot data center. The data-processing environment consisted of IBM, HP, and Prime mainframes. Also developed plans to begin and design, install, and implement interconnections among the various mainframes using Ethernet and IBM Token Ring. Reviewed a backbone network consisting of two fiber-optic rings connecting data center to a primary and backup central office.

Major Accounting Firm

Designed the new data center for a large professional accounting firm. This assignment resulted in layouts for network control center for voice and data, the hardware components (CPUs, disk drives, backup drives), console area, printer pool, and tape library, and development of requirements for hardware vendors, engineers, and architects.

Major Medical Center

Responsible for the evaluation of several potential data center site locations. This assignment included evaluating communications, transportation facilities, electrical power quality, availability of personnel, safety, and personal services (e.g., restaurants, shopping, banking, parking).

PRIOR EXPERIENCE IN DATA DEVELOPMENT

Before joining the Data Processing Group of Western Consulting Associates, Mr. Chee served as Senior Data Manager for a major commercial bank. His accomplishments include the following:

- Managed a large-scale data center operations department composed of four server-scale processors, supporting over 700 online users. Functional areas of responsibility were:
    - Network scheduling and control center
    - Consoles
    - Printer pool
    - Tape pool/tape library
    - COM lab
    - Operation technicians
    - Remote job entry sites
    - Library maintenance and control
- Planned and controlled the budget, hardware, and personnel expenses for the data center. Major accomplishments were:
    - Planned and installed all online users' communication hardware
    - Planned and installed remote job entry sites
    - Reduced staff by means of changes in work flow, purchase of labor-saving products, and conversion of tab equipment processing to the mainframe
    - Planned and coordinated major processor and operating system upgrades
- As a member of the online technical support group, during the relocation of the bank's data center he was responsible for:
    - Design of the network control center
    - Development of plans for installation testing of all data communications equipment
    - Maintenance of the online monitor
    - Support of online applications support programmers
    - Development of in-house code to perform restart/recovery for online applications

Armstrong & Hou Financial, Inc.
Data Center Design   A. Carla Washington

A. CARLA WASHINGTON

Ms. Washington is a senior consultant with the Information Services Group of Western Consulting Associates. As a consultant, Ms. Washington specializes in management information systems. She received her BA degree from Pennsylvania State University and her MBA degree from the University of Pittsburgh. Ms. Washington has 15 years of data processing experience. Her primary areas of expertise are in the management of information systems, warehousing and distribution, and cost accounting and statistical analysis.

MAJOR PROFESSIONAL ACCOMPLISHMENTS

As a consultant, Ms. Washington recently completed the following projects:
- Computer center design and relocation planning for several companies including:
  - Three major brokerage firms
  - Major financial services firm
  - Two major pharmaceutical firms
  - Three medium-sized manufacturing firms
  - Major bank
  - Two large medical centers
- Overall reviews of data-processing activities and centralization/decentralization studies for several organizations including the following:
  - A European multinational electronics and appliance manufacturer
  - A multibillion-dollar diverse conglomerate
  - A leading commodities trading company
  - A major southern electric utility
  - A large public housing authority
- Company capacity planning/hardware acquisition engagements for several organizations including the following:
  - A leading investment trading corporation
  - A major conglomerate
  - A major southwestern utility company
  - A multinational electronics and appliance manufacturer

- A major Middle Atlantic bank
- Two large medical centers

PRIOR DATA PROCESSING EXPERIENCE

Prior to her consulting career, Ms. Washington successfully planned and executed three computer center relocations as follows:

United States Steel Corporation

The Western Regional Data Center was moved and merged into the Central Regional Data Center. In the process all hardware in the Central RDC was replaced, as was all operating system software. Ms. Washington's specific responsibilities were technical planning, configuration definition, and technical troubleshooting for the first year of operation of the new site.

Bankers Trust Company

Ms. Washington had primary responsibility for relocating the bank's main computer center from Wall Street to a new operations building at 1 Bankers Trust Plaza. Her responsibilities included development of the configuration of hardware, overall logistical planning for and execution of the physical move, and definition of and installation of teleprocessing equipment. She achieved the following:

- Cutover was complete within 24 hours with no disruption to the user community.
- Move was completed on schedule and under budget.
- Computer center was fully backed up.
- Configurations developed included three large-scale mainframes, disc units, backup library, and 500-line teleprocessing network.

Scholastic, Inc.

Ms. Washington had overall responsibility for information systems as well as warehousing and distribution responsibilities when she relocated Scholastic's information center from northern New Jersey to the Meadowlands. This relocation involved four medium-scale mainframes and 250 clerical and professional personnel.

The move was completed over a three-day holiday with no disruption to business and was accomplished on time and under budget.

Appendix D

Brief Guide to International Business English

Today, there is a greater chance that your proposal will be read by clients or executives who speak English as a second language. An RFP might come from a company in South America, Europe, Asia, or the Middle East. Or executives from other countries may be working for a U.S. firm and be asked to review your proposal. You will need to adjust your writing to accommodate those who are not native English speakers. The four basic tips in this appendix will help you write proposal documents that your international clients can read and understand more easily.

Four Tips for International Business Writing

Although English has become the international business language of the world, people still speak and read English through the filters of their culture and native languages. When they learn English, they must learn a new vocabulary, a new word order, and a new culture.

For example, we are used to a particular word order in English. Modifiers usually come before the words they modify (*offshore platform*), and subjects usually come before verbs (the *vice president* will speak). Foreign languages use different word orders to convey meaning. Modifiers will follow the words they modify, and subjects may come after the verbs. For example:

> *English:* We received your registered package in the mail.
> *German:* We received in the mail a package registered.
> *Chinese:* Received we package mail registered.
> *Spanish:* We received your package registered in the mail.

When nonnative English speakers read documents in English, they have two tasks: understanding the English vocabulary and understanding English word order. Your job is to make those tasks as easy for them as possible. At the same time, you don't want to sound as if you're writing for fourth graders. You want to simplify your language without sounding simple-minded, and you want to inform your readers without insulting their intelligence. This means you have to think carefully not only about *what* you say but about *how* you say it.

Following are four tips for revising your language for nonnative English readers:

1. Simplify your sentence structure.
2. Keep your verb tenses and verbs simple.
3. Avoid the use of idioms, slang, jargon, and cultural references.
4. Group your ideas into shorter paragraphs and lists and use graphics when possible.

Simplify Your Sentence Structure

When you are writing for nonnative English speakers, the general rule is *keep the sentence structure simple.* The more clauses and phrases you add to a sentence, the greater your chances of being misunderstood. For example:

Complex: The new system, *which is linked to cloud computing,* will allow users to download files, *even large graphic files,* much faster *than it used to take them.* [The basic meaning of this sentence is, "The new system allows users to download files much faster." The complex sentence structure obscures that message.]

Simplified: The new system is linked to cloud computing. Users can download even large graphic files much faster. [The sentences are shorter and simpler; readers focus on the content and not on the complex sentence structure.]

Keep these guidelines in mind when revising your sentences:

- *Avoid using several phrases and clauses in the same sentence.* As shown in the example above, phrases and clauses make a sentence harder to understand.

- *Break long sentences into two or three shorter ones.* Make sure a sentence presents only one or two main ideas. You want the reader to understand each point, especially if you are trying to persuade him or her to accept your proposal and hire your company.

- *Use transition words to help readers follow your thinking.* Transition words include, "first, second," "finally," "as a result," "therefore," "for example," "next," "also," "in addition," and so on. These words help clarify the logical connections among ideas in your sentences.

In the following passage, the writer tries to explain why a company's products are losing market share.

We understand that Hyperion's major video game line, which last year had 40 percent of the market, has lost considerable market share—the first time the company has experienced a loss since it was founded [sentence too complex, presents too many ideas]. The reasons for the loss in market share are cloud computing in the United States and new animations that other countries have developed over the past five years to change the way video games are played [sentence too long and confusing]. New 3-D gaming technology has been developed by Advaitya Games in India. More companies in the United States and Europe are adopting this new technology and writing new games for the platforms. Companies that use old technologies are quickly losing market share [transition words missing between these sentences].

Here is the same passage revised:

We understand that Hyperion's major video game line has lost considerable market share for the first time in the company's history. Last year, Hyperion had 40 percent of the gaming market. This year it has only 25 percent of the market. [major problem is stated clearly]. The reasons for the loss in market share are clear to those who follow developments in the industry. Over the past five years, cloud computing in the United States and new animations from other countries have changed the way video games are played [shorter sentences are easier to understand]. Advaitya Games in India, for example, has developed a new 3-D gaming technology. Today, more companies in the United States and Europe are adopting this technology and writing games for the new platforms. As a result, companies that use old technologies are quickly losing market share [transition words, "for example," "Today," "As a result" clarify connections between ideas in sentences].

One way to check for overloaded or lengthy sentences is to read aloud a page or two of your work. Or ask someone who is a nonnative English speaker to read your work. It should quickly become clear which sentences are too long or too complex and need to be revised.

Keep Your Verb Tenses and Verbs Simple

English has a wealth of verb tenses to talk about the past, present, and future. That very wealth can cause problems for nonnative English speakers, especially those from Asia and Africa.

Use Time Cues with Verb Tenses.
Many non-Western languages have only one tense—the present—and depend entirely on context to clarify the sequence of past, present, and future. In these languages, the following sentences are perfectly correct:

Present: I *send* the memo this morning.
Past: I already *send* the memo yesterday.
Future: I *send* the memo tomorrow.
Past and future: I *send* the memo yesterday and then tomorrow
    I *send* a follow-up memo.

Notice that the verb *send* never changes its form. All time cues are given by the context, or surrounding words.

In English, we signal changes in time by changing or adding to the verb:

Present: I'm the one who *sends* the memos.

Past: I *sent* the memo this morning. (The verb *sent* signals that this action took place in the past. "This morning" tells more specifically *when* in the past.)

Past: I *had* already *sent* the memo when he *called*. (*Had sent* signals that this action took place in the more distant past.)

Future: I *will send* the memo tomorrow.

Past and future: I *sent* the memo yesterday, and tomorrow I *will send* a follow-up memo.

When you have a sequence of actions that covers a span of time, describe the actions in a series of shorter sentences. Use context cues to start the sentences.

Original: I *sent* the memo with all the specifications yesterday, and we *will discuss* the details tomorrow with the architects.

Revised: Yesterday, I sent the memo with all the specifications. *Tomorrow,* we will discuss the details with the architects.

These changes clarify the sequence—"yesterday" and "tomorrow." Readers know *when* an action happened or will happen. Now they can focus on understanding the action described in each sentence.

Use Simpler Verb Forms.

In English, we use complex verb forms without realizing how difficult they may be for a nonnative speaker to understand. For example:

Complex: We *would have liked to include* more precise cost estimates in our proposal. However, the price of raw materials *has proved to be* too unpredictable at this time.

Simpler: Unfortunately, we *cannot include* more precise cost estimates in our proposal. The price of raw materials *is* too unpredictable at this time.

The verb forms "would have liked to include" and "has proved to be" obscure the meaning of the sentence. "Would have liked to include" means "cannot include." If you can't do something, it's better to say so directly. Also, the phrase "has proved to be" simply means that something "is."

The following lists provide examples for some of the more common complex verb structures and their substitutes. After a while, you will begin to catch these complex verbs in your own writing and change them to simpler forms.

Avoid	*Use Instead*
would have liked to...	cannot...
will be managing...	will manage...
had been using...	used...
has been extensively improved...	is greatly improved...
might have been able to work...	might have worked...
is able to bring...	can bring...

Use One-Word Verbs instead of Phrasal Verbs.

Verbs used with prepositions (*take on, speak up, take advantage of*) are known as "phrasal verbs" and can present problems for nonnative English speakers. Whenever possible, substitute one-word verbs for these phrasal verbs.

> *Phrasal verb:* I will *speak to* the issues outlined in this proposal.
> *One-word verb:* I will *discuss* the issues outlined in this proposal.

Look over the list below of common phrasal verbs and their substitutes. If you spot phrasal verbs in your own writing, try to find one-word substitutes to use instead.

Avoid	*Use Instead*
take issue with	disagree
make clear	clarify, explain
look at	examine
shut out	exclude
keep abreast of	monitor, track

talk over	discuss
keep on track	supervise, monitor
bring up (an issue)	raise
turn down (an offer)	decline
turn down (the sound)	lower

If you cannot avoid using a phrasal verb, keep the words together. The reader will have a better chance of understanding what you mean.

> *Confusing: Spell* the name of every company *out.* (The reader might wonder what "out" refers to.)
> *Clear: Spell out* the name of every company.
> *Confusing:* We will have to *turn* the power grid *off* during the test.
> *Clear:* We will have to *turn off* the power grid during the test.

Use Active instead of Passive Voice.

The passive voice puts the actor last in a sentence and places the emphasis on *what* was done, not on *who* did it (*The contract was sent by me*). The passive voice automatically adds words to your verbs. Compare these two sentences:

> *Active voice:* Our company *will provide* three solutions to the problem.
> *Passive voice:* Three solutions to the problem *will be provided* by our company.

In general, the passive voice simply adds more words to your sentences. Look over the examples below of passive and active voices. Whenever possible, change passive voice to active voice in your writing. The active voice also tells the reader *who* or *what* is responsible for the action.

Avoid Passive Voice	*Use Active Voice Instead*
letters are being written	we are writing letters
team will be managed	the project leader will manage
results had been reported	the company reported the results

Exception: The passive voice is useful when you need to be diplomatic. For example, suppose one of your clients made a serious error in submitting specifications to you for a new power system. You might point this out by using the diplomatic passive voice:

Diplomatic passive voice: We found that an error *had been made* in the original specifications we received. (No blame is assigned for the error.)

Avoid Idioms, Slang, Jargon, and Cultural References

It's natural to believe that everyone understands the idioms, slang, jargon, and cultural references of the English language. But nonnative speakers have not grown up hearing or reading these forms of expression and either tend to take them literally or fail to understand them at all. Your job is to find a more straightforward way of explaining what you mean.

- *Idioms:* Figures of speech or expressions such as "above board," "back to square one," "call it a day," or, "keep posted." Nonnative speakers will tend to take these expressions literally and miss your intended meaning.
- *Slang:* Words or expressions that are part of popular speech, such as "wipeout," "no-brainer," or "cut a deal." These words are too casual and imprecise to be used in formal writing. Whenever they appear, delete them and find a better word or words.
- *Jargon:* Words used in a particular industry or field, such as in the finance industry: "Roth IRA," "call put," "P/E ratio," or, "IRR." Many of your readers will not be experts in the technical aspects of an industry or business and will not understand jargon terms. Keep these terms to a minimum and define them when you first use them in a document.
- *Cultural references:* Concepts, sayings, or terms that require a deeper knowledge of a culture to understand. For example, a reference to "March Madness" would make little sense unless you knew that it referred to the national college basketball competition that occurs each year in March.

To catch these forms of expression in your writing, you will need to become more aware of how you think, speak, and write. For example, the paragraph below is from the first draft of a proposal in response to the RFP from an international food manufacturer:

> Rycorp Foods is one of the world's leading manufacturers of artificial sweeteners with its major headquarters in Sao Paulo, Brazil. Rycorp would like *to break into* the middle-level restaurant market in the United States. The company wants to learn about the market as well as the major competition it would face *from the get-go*. Most middle-level restaurants purchase food products from *co-ops* or *brokers*, who negotiate between suppliers and restaurant buyers. Sometimes these brokers are in one location that resembles a *strip mall* of food products. At *every step along the way* in the purchasing process, buyers and suppliers must conform to *HACCP* protocols to ensure safe handling of food or food products.

The terms in italics are all based on expressions or cultural references used in the United States. Below is the same paragraph revised to follow guidelines for international business English:

> Rycorp Foods is one of the world's leading manufacturers of artificial sweeteners with its major headquarters in Sao Paulo, Brazil. Rycorp would like *to enter* [idiom deleted] the middle-level restaurant market in the United States. The company wants to learn about the market *and about its major competitors* [no need to add any more words]. Most middle-level restaurants purchase food products from *agents, known as co-operatives or brokers* [define the terms], who negotiate between suppliers and restaurant buyers. Sometimes these agents *occupy a single location where they sell to different restaurant buyers* [delete unnecessary cultural reference; explain setup in more detail]. At *every point* [idiom deleted] in the purchasing process, buyers and suppliers must comply with *government regulations* [*HACCP* is "hazard analysis and critical control point" and would not mean much to a foreign company] to ensure safe handling of food or food products.

One of the easiest ways to catch idioms, slang, jargon, or cultural references in your writing is to ask nonnative English speakers to read your work and point out what they don't understand. This exercise can give you valuable insights regarding the culture-based expressions and references in your writing.

Use Short Paragraphs, Numbered and Bulleted Lists, and Graphics

In addition to simplifying your language, you can also help your readers by simplifying the way you present information on the page. At times, you will need to give the reader instructions, a sequence of steps, or a series of items. You can group this information into easy-to-read short paragraphs or numbered or bulleted lists. Where possible, use graphics to illustrate your ideas and to reinforce your major points.

Notice how the following passage can be reformatted to make the material easier for the reader to understand.

Original.
The project consists of two phases. Phase I—Data Center Design—consists of five steps in the design process. We will need to develop detailed space requirements, review data center hardware, evaluate the pros and cons of different layouts, prepare data center blueprints, and have weekly progress meetings with the client. Phase II—Data Center Construction—consists of three steps. We will need to prepare all architectural and engineering blueprints, review our work with the client, and present the final blueprints and specifications to the contractors.

Short Paragraphs.
The project consists of two phases. Phase I—Data Center Design—consists of five steps. We will need to develop detailed space requirements, review data center hardware, evaluate the pros and cons of different layouts, prepare data center blueprints, and have weekly progress meetings with the client.

Phase II—Data Center Construction—consists of three steps. We will need to prepare all architectural and engineering blueprints, review our work with the client, and present the final blueprints and specifications to the contractors.

Numbered List.

The project consists of two phases. Phase I—Data Center Design—consists of five steps:

1. Develop detailed space requirements.
2. Review data center hardware.
3. Evaluate the pros and cons of different layouts.
4. Prepare preliminary blueprints.
5. Have weekly progress meetings with the client.

Phase II—Data Center Construction—consists of three steps:

1. Prepare all final architectural and engineering blueprints.
2. Review our work with the client.
3. Present the final blueprints and specifications to the contractors.

Bulleted List.

The project consists of two phases. Phase I—Data Center Design—consists of the following steps:

- Develop detailed space requirements.
- Review data center hardware.
- Evaluate the pros and cons of different layouts.
- Prepare preliminary blueprints.
- Have weekly progress meetings with the client.

Phase II—Data Center Construction—consists of three steps:

- Prepare all final architectural and engineering blueprints.
- Review our work with the client.
- Present the final blueprints and specifications to the contractors.

Graphics.

The information in this passage could also be presented as a flow chart.

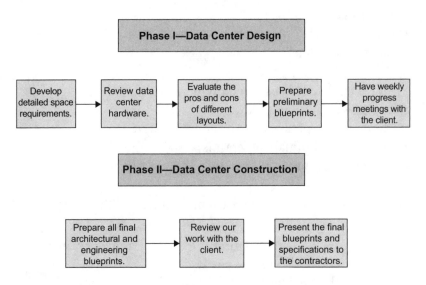

Summary

Keep in mind that nonnative English speakers must not only master a foreign vocabulary but also a foreign word order and foreign cultural references and expressions. Your job is to make it as easy as possible for them to understand your written documents.

Follow these basic international business English guidelines to write or revise your written communications:

1. Simplify your sentence structure.
    - Avoid using several clauses and phrases in the same sentence.
    - Break long sentences into two or three shorter ones.
    - Use transition words to help readers follow your thinking.
2. Keep your verbs and verb tenses simple.
    - Use time cues with verb tenses ("today," "yesterday," "next week").
    - Use simpler verb forms.
    - Use one-word verbs instead of phrasal verbs.
    - Use the active instead of the passive voice.

3. Avoid idioms, slang, jargon, and cultural references in your writing.
4. Use short paragraphs, numbered or bulleted lists, and graphics to present your ideas.

Your goal is to simplify your language without sounding simple-minded and to inform your readers without insulting their intelligence.

Additional aids to your writing are presented in Appendix E: Frequently Confused Words (such as *affect, effect*) and Appendix F: Frequently Misspelled Words (such as *interfere,* which is often misspelled as *interfer*).

Appendix E
Frequently Confused Words

The meaning and spelling of the following words are commonly confused. Practice using them until the correct usage is familiar to you.

accept, except
accept—to take, agree
I accept the offer.
except—excluding, omitting
Everyone left *except* me.

advice, advise
advice—opinion, counsel
She needs your *advice*.
advise—to counsel
Please *advise* him of his rights.

affect, effect
affect—to influence, change
Inflation always *affects* our level of income.
effect—(n.) impression, result; (v.) to cause
The computer has had a profound *effect* on our everyday lives. It has *effected* a complete change in the way we do business.

already, all ready
already—even now
We *already* have a robot.
all ready—all prepared
They're *all ready* to go.

assent, ascent
assent—(v.) to agree; (n.) permission
Did they *assent* to your request? The entire board gave its *assent* to the project.
ascent—movement upward
On the third day, they made their *ascent* to the top of Mount Everest.

capital, capitol
capital—seat of government; wealth
The nation's *capital* braced itself for the holiday weekend.
We need more *capital* to finance our new product line.
capitol—government building
They are putting a new roof on the *capitol*.

cite, site, sight
cite—refer to, state
I *cited* my reasons for disagreeing.
site—location
The *site* for our home is lovely.
sight—scene
The city at dawn is a beautiful *sight*.

cloths, clothes
cloths—pieces of cloth
Use soft *cloths* for polishing your silver.
clothes—wearing apparel
Every spring he buys new *clothes* and throws out the old ones.

complement, compliment
complement—something that completes
Her humor is the perfect *complement* to my pessimism.
compliment—to say something good about someone; a flattering remark

My father always *compliments* my mother on her painting.
The boss's *compliment* meant a lot to Carl.

compose, comprise
compose—to form by putting together (used with "*of*")
The committee is *composed of* two senior managers and one consultant.
comprise—to be formed or made up by (not used with the preposition "*of*")
The committee *comprises* two senior managers and one consultant.
Incorrect: The committee *is comprised of...*

consul, council, counsel
consul—foreign embassy official
The Swedish *consul* threw a party for the president.
council—official body
The city *council* passed the ordinance by a three-to-one margin.
counsel—(v.) to advise; (n.) legal advisor
Find someone to *counsel* you about your accident. In fact, you should hire the company lawyer to act as *counsel* in this matter.

dissent, descent, descend
dissent—disagreement
Mine was the only vote in *dissent* of the proposed amendment.
descent—a decline, fall
The road made a sharp *descent* and then curved dangerously to the right.
descend—to come down
They had to *descend* from the mountaintop in darkness.

fewer, less
fewer—used for individual units, numbers
You will have to make *fewer* mistakes or order more erasers.
We have five *fewer* doughnuts than we had this morning.
less—used for general quantities
The amount of money in our bank account is *less* than it was last year.

formerly, formally
formerly—previously

I was *formerly* a recruiter.
formally—officially
She was sworn in *formally* as the fifth member of the panel.

imply, infer
imply—to suggest
Are you *implying* that I was at the scene of the crime?
infer—to deduce from evidence
Your gloves were found in the room; therefore, we *infer* that you
visited the deceased sometime last night.

it's, its
it's—contraction of **it is** or **it has**
It's [it has] been a long day.
I've seen the play; *it's* [it is] not very good.
its—possessive form of the pronoun *it*
When the ship fired *its* guns, the blast was deafening.

later, latter
later—after a time
They'll mail it *later* today.
latter—last mentioned of the two
If it's a choice between the beach and the mountains, I'll take the
latter.

lead, led, lead
lead—(v.) to go before; (adj.) first
The boys always *lead* the rush to the beach.
The *lead* singer seems off tonight.
led—(v., past tense of **lead**) went before
They *led* the parade playing their kazoos.
lead—(n.) heavy metal; graphite
This paperweight is made of *lead*.

lie, lay
lie—to rest or recline (lie, lay, lain)
The cat always *lies* down on my sweater. Yesterday he *lay* on it all
day. I wish he had *lain* somewhere else.

lay—to put or place something (lay, laid, laid)
I will *lay* the sweater on the couch. Yesterday I *laid* it there without thinking about the cat. I have *laid* it there many times.

lose, loose, loss
lose—misplace
Don't *lose* the tickets.
loose—not fastened down; release
The screw is *loose* on the showerhead.
Turn the kids *loose* in the park.
loss—deprivation
His leaving was a *loss* to the company.

past, passed
past—(n., adj.) preceding
The *past* president gave the gavel to the new president.
passed—(v., past tense of **pass**) went by; gone by
We *passed* my cousin on the road.

personal, personnel
personal—relating to or affecting an individual
Can I ask you a *personal* question?
personnel—a department; workers
The human resources (*personnel*) office keeps records on all company *personnel*.

precede, proceed
precede—to come before
My older brother *precedes* me by one grade in school.
proceed—to go ahead
We can *proceed* with our game as soon as the weather clears.

principle, principal
principle—rule, standard
Sound *principles* can help you make good decisions.
principal—(adj.) main, chief; (n.) superintendent
She is the state's *principal* witness in this case.
I'll never forget my grade school *principal*, Mr. Harvey.

quiet, quite
quiet—silent
The valley is *quiet* at dusk.
quite—completely; to a considerable degree
He was *quite* upset with himself for losing the race.
I *quite* agree that the judge was unfair.

rise, raise
rise—(v.) to go up, to get up; (n.) reaction
The moon *rises* later each night.
Your statement to the governor certainly got a *rise* out of him.
raise—(v.) to lift, bring up; (n.) an increase
Raise the picture a little higher.
After four months, he finally got a *raise* in pay.

sit, set
sit—to rest in an upright position
We had to *sit* on the plane for three hours before we took off.
set—to put or place something
They *set* the coffee on the table.
She *set* the files in order.

stationary, stationery
stationary—still, fixed
The chair is *stationary*.
stationery—letter paper
He took out a sheet of *stationery* and wrote a letter.

than, then
than—after a comparison
Vivian is taller *than* Kelly.
then—next; in that case
She took Fred's order and *then* mine.
If you want to skip the mashed potatoes, *then* have the waitress mark
it on the order.

that, which
that—used to introduce a phrase or clause essential to the meaning
of the sentence; not set off by commas

The shipment *that* arrived yesterday had to be returned. (*That arrived yesterday* identifies which shipment had to be returned and is essential information.)

We ate the 15 doughnuts *that* Jan brought to work this morning.

which—used to refer to a specific noun or pronoun and to introduce a phrase or clause not essential to the meaning of the sentence; usually set off by commas

We ate 15 doughnuts, *which* was 15 too many. (*Which* refers to *doughnuts* and adds additional information—*which was 15 too many*—that is not essential to the meaning of the sentence.)

The shipment, *which* arrived yesterday, had to be returned. (*Which arrived yesterday* is incidental information and is set off by commas.)

Exception: that or *which* can at times be used interchangeably to avoid too many repetitions of either word in a sentence.

there, their, they're
there—a place
The book has to be on the table; I saw it *there* just a minute ago.
their—possessive form of *they*
Why don't they take *their* skateboards and go home?
they're—contraction of *they are*
They're upset that the watermelon fell off the table.

weather, whether
weather—climate
The *weather* has been warming slowly over the past 50 years.
whether—if; regardless
They have to know *whether* you are going. You should go with them *whether* you feel like it or not.

who's, whose
who's—contraction of *who is* or *who has*
Do you know *who's* [who is] coming to the party tonight? No, I don't know *who's* [who has] been invited.
whose—possessive form of *who*
Whose purple car is parked outside our house?

you're, your
you're—contraction of *you are*
You're going to be late for dinner.
your—possessive form of *you*
Your dinner is cold.

Appendix F
Frequently Misspelled Words

The following list contains words that are frequently misspelled.
Use this list as a quick reference in addition to consulting a good
dictionary.

abbreviate
absence
abundant
accessible
accidentally
accommodate
accompanies
accompaniment
accumulate
accuracy
acknowledgment
acquaintance
adequately
admission
admittance
adolescent
advantageous
allege
alliance
analysis

analyze
anonymous
apologetically
apparatus
apparent
appreciate
appropriate
argument
arrangement
arrears
ascertain
association
attendance
authorize
auxiliary
awfully

ballet
bankruptcy

beneficial
bibliography
bookkeeper
boulevard
brochure
buffet
bulletin

calculation
calendar
camouflage
canceled/cancelled
cancellation
catalog/catalogue
catastrophe
category
cellar
cemetery
changeable
choose
chose
colossal
column
commitment
committed
committee
comparative
competent
competition
competitor
complexion
comptroller
conceivable
concise
conscience
conscientious
consciousness
consensus
consistency

contingency
controlling
controversy
correspondence
correspondents
criticize
curriculum

debacle
debtor
decadent
deceitful
deference
deferred
dependent
depreciation
description
desirable
detrimental
dilemma
diligence
disastrous
disciple
discrimination
dissatisfied
division

economical
ecstasy
effect
efficiency
embarrassment
emphasize
endeavor
enforceable
enormous
enthusiastically
entrance
espionage

exaggerate
excel
exceptionally
exhaustion
exhibition
exhibitor
exhilaration
existence
exorbitant
expensive
extension
exuberant

facilitate
familiar
familiarize
fascination
feasible
feminine
financier
flip chart
foreign
forfeit
franchise
fraud
fraudulent
freight
fulfill

gauge
grammar
grievance
guarantee
guaranty
guidance

harassment
hereditary
hindrance

horizontal
hygiene
hypocrisy
hypothetical

ideally
idiomatic
illegible
immediately
imperative
implement
incidentally
inconvenience
indemnity
independent
indispensable
inevitable
inflationary
influential
ingenious
initial
initiative
innocent
inoculate
institution
intellectual
interfere
interference
interpretation
interrupt
invoice
irrelevant
irresistible
itemize
itinerary

jeopardize
jeopardy
judgment/judgement

kerosene
knowledge
knowledgeable

labeled
laborious
larynx
legitimate
leisurely
liable
license
likelihood
livelihood
liquor
livable
loose
lose
lucrative
luxurious

magistrate
magnificence
maintenance
majestic
malicious
manageable
mandatory
maneuver
marketable
marriageable
martyrdom
materialism
measurable
mediator
mediocre
melancholy
metaphor
miniature
miscellaneous

mischievous
misspell
misstatement
mortgage
mosquito
municipal
mysterious

naive
necessity
negligible
negotiate
neurotic
neutral
ninety
ninth
noticeable

objectionable
observant
occasionally
occupant
occurrence
omission
omitting
opinionated
opportunity
option
outrageous
overrated

pageant
pamphlet
parallel
paralysis
parity
parliament
particularly
pastime
pedestal

penicillin
permanent
permissible
permitted
persistent
personal
perspiration
phenomenon
physician
picnicking
plausible
pneumonia
politician
possession
practically
precede
precise
preference
preferred
prejudice
presence
prestige
presumption
prevalent
privilege
procedure
propaganda
prophesy
prove
psychoanalysis
psychology
pursue

qualitative
quality
quantitative
quantity
questionnaire
quietly

quit
quite

rebellion
receive
recommend
recommendation
reconciliation
recurrence
reducible
reference
referred
rehearsal
reimburse
relieve
reminiscent
remittance
remitted
repetition
representative
resource
respectfully
responsibility
returnable
reveal
revenue
routine

salable/saleable
schedule
scientific
scrutinize
separation
sergeant
serviceable
siege
significant
similar
souvenir
specifically

specimen
sponsor
statistics
strategic
stubbornness
substantial
succeed
succession
superficial
superfluous
superintendent
supersede
supervisor
suppress
surroundings
susceptible
symbolic
symmetrical
synonymous

tariff
technician
temperature
tendency
theoretical
tolerance
tomorrow
traffic
tragedy
transcend
transmit
transmittal
transparent
tried
twelfth
tyranny

unanimous
undoubtedly

uniform
universal
unmistakable
unnatural
unnecessary
unscrupulous

vaccine
vacuum
variation
vehicle
vengeance
ventilation
versatile
vigilance
villain
vinegar
volume

waive
warranty
welcome
whisper
whistle
whiteboard
wholly
withhold

yacht
yawn
yield
young
youth

zealous
zenith

Index

About the Authors

Robert J. Hamper worked for AT&T for over 11 years in such areas as market analysis, economic evaluation, market management, strategic planning, and financial management. He also designed and implemented practical applications of portfolio theory and optimization modeling of resource allocation in the strategic market/planning process.

Prior to working at AT&T, Mr. Hamper worked at Bell Laboratories where he developed several intricate financial/marketing models and applications. He also wrote testimonies to the Illinois Commerce Commission, Federal Communication Commission, and the Justice Department. Mr. Hamper is president of his own consulting firm, which specializes in strategic planning, and he has been a consultant for over 18 years to Fortune 500 and midsized corporations. He has been court-appointed to a provisional board of directors to oversee restructuring of firms on the verge of bankruptcy.

He holds BSBA and MBA degrees from Illinois State University and is ABD at Northern Illinois University. He has been a full-time and adjunct professor in the Graduate School of Business at Dominican University and Loyola University of Chicago. He has also presented papers in the fields of finance and marketing to professional organizations. Mr. Hamper has refereed marketing, economics, and statistics texts for major U.S. publishers.

L. Sue Baugh is an independent business writer who has developed, edited, or contributed to numerous texts in marketing, finance, economics, management, risk management, human resources, and business communications. Clients include Scott Foresman, Longman Publishing, Rand McNally, McGraw-Hill, Prentice Hall, Houghton Mifflin Harcourt, National Restaurant Association, and American College of Emergency Physicians.

Ms. Baugh worked for six years as senior editor at Booz, Allen & Hamilton, Inc., one of the world's largest management consultant firms. As part of the firm's report production department, she played an integral role in developing proposals to respond to bids from industry, government, and nonprofit associations.

Ms. Baugh also has taught in-house classes in proposal and report writing to new consultants, preparing them for the challenges of the management consultant field. In addition, she has helped native and nonnative English speakers learn the basics of international business English to improve their written communications.